# FOR THE LOVE OF DESIGN

## ESSAYS BY STEVEN HELLER

**ALLWORTH PRESS**
NEW YORK

Allworth Press books may be purchased in bulk at special discounts for sales promotion, corporate gifts, fund-raising, or educational purposes. Special editions can also be created to specifications. For details, contact the Special Sales Department, Allworth Press, 307 West 36th Street, 11th Floor, New York, NY 10018 or info@skyhorsepublishing.com.

26 25 24 23 22     5 4 3 2 1

Published by Allworth Press, an imprint of Skyhorse Publishing, Inc. 307 West 36th Street, 11th Floor, New York, NY 10018. Allworth Press® is a registered trademark of Skyhorse Publishing, Inc.®, a Delaware corporation.

www.allworth.com

Cover and interior design by Ezra Lee

Library of Congress Cataloging-in-Publication Data is available on file.

Print ISBN: 978-1-62153-809-7
eBook ISBN: 978-1-62153-810-3

Printed in the United States of America

# 5. CONVERSATIONS

# 6. TYPE LOVE

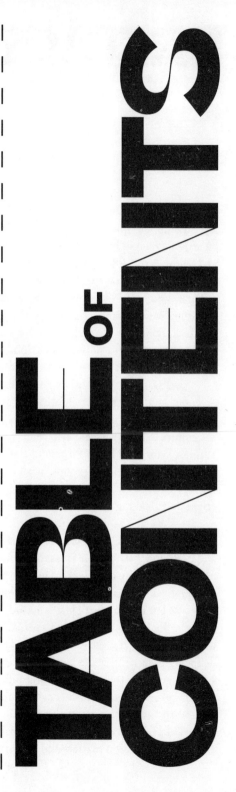

# PREFACE

- - - - - - - - - - - - - - - - - - - - - - - - -

I began writing about illustration, graphic commentary, and satiric art history and contemporary practice in the mid-1970s. Many of the artists I covered were also poster artists, typographers and graphic designers, so an interest in graphic design developed, and by the early 1980s I was deeply involved in exploring, analyzing, and critiquing visual culture. At that time there were a sizable number of magazine and newspaper outlets—and books—for my essays and feature stories on the roles that all manner of "communication graphics" played in the popular, political, cultural, and social worlds. I produced hundreds of articles from interviews to profiles, from surveys to concept stories, from lengthy to short profiles of persons, places, and things—often as many as two or three stories a week for over three dozen years.

I was not the only design writer of my ilk, but there were very few of us in the seventies and early to mid-eighties. Most bona fide art historians and critics kept their distance, although a few entered the design world through the back door—and covered the commercial artists who also were "fine" artists (of which there were many from William Morris to Pablo Picasso to Barbara Kruger). Most of the design writing itself fell stylistically into two groups: academic and trade. The former was laden with jargon meant to be understood by a small group of scholars. The latter was more technical or celebratory, leaving very little room for criticism.

When I began writing I did not attempt to avoid these two extremes. I admit to writing my share of pseudo-academicism for which I had little training or patience—and only ended that when I was told point-blank by a respected designer that she could not understand a word I was saying. At first, I took it as a compliment in support of my deliberate aloofness yet I realized that my real purpose was not to make an exclusionary language but to reach people of all kinds and to make design less rarified than it was.

Thanks in large part to *PRINT* magazine's editor, Martin Fox, I began to develop a personal voice in the primarily trade-oriented design press. Sometimes it was deliberately contentious to kick up some dust, other times it was purely informational. I usually allowed the story itself to guide how and with what levels of observation, reportage, or critique I would cover a subject. For instance, I wrote on aesthetics in general and aesthetics as a political tool. I enjoyed discovering connections between graphic design and other art and cultural forms. I reveled in writing about forgotten and unknown design masters and their respective schools, movements, or plain old relationships. Since as popular culture, graphic design has as many links to the past as every other integral art form, I found endless revelations and connotations to work with. Stories about design, designers, and their impact on our lives were abundant.

I often claimed that graphic design subjects provided me with an endless supply of fascinating themes. Paul Rand said "Design is Everywhere," and I'll add that everything can be narrated through a design perspective. With that in mind, I came up with dozens of story ideas a week. Some were obvious, others not. Some were easy to tell, others were more difficult to get the story right.

I feel fortunate to have come of age during—and perhaps even contributed to—the growth of graphic design journalism. The "trade magazines" that had hegemony of design writing for so long—since before the turn of the century—were beginning to be complemented and supplemented by new design voices. Print was not the first, but it arguably led the charge from exclusively professional news to intellectual and deep-dive journalism. But the others quickly followed suit.

I did my share of purely professional articles but each year design magazines were looking for a happy editorial balance between industry concerns, profiles, and social commentary. I'd like to think I played a significant role in changing the tone and direction of design journals. And while this has become more relevant with the advent of blogs, it began in print and continues there as well. I am also proud to say that I certainly helped in making graphic design more visible and accessible in mainstream periodicals and newspapers.

I have contributed hundreds of stories to everything from *Baseline* to the *New York Times* (and now a lot online, including *The Daily Heller*, a blog I have done for the past seven or more years). It is not being modest to say that I may have abetted in raising the public's consciousness of those assemblages of type and image, often called visual communications, to a larger and more appreciative audience. Although some of my topics are admittedly arcane or eccentric, I have done my best to make this field understandable to those in and out of it. (The AIGA has even named their annual critical and cultural design writing award in my name. One of my proudest honors.)

I have not done this alone. In everything I have done, the editors have made my words better and designers have framed my stories in order to best capture the reader's attention. For making my words worth reading I thank them all.

# FOR THE

# LOV
# DES

---

## ESSAYS BY

# STEVEN

E OF

IGN

- - - - - - - - - - - - - - -

HELLER

# PART 1:
# WISDOM

# HELLO GRADS (2021)

**E**ach year I prepare an original graduation commencement speech on the off chance that some art and design school, somewhere, would invite me to a last-minute fill-in. I've received zero calls in over ten years but the following persistently continues the tradition (and it is free for those interested in my words of wisdom).

Greetings Class of . . .

You've heard it a lot: This has been an unprecedented year. Although warned that the odds of a pandemic are high, our leaders on the whole had chosen to ignore caution.

So, here we are, for a second graduation, sitting in front of our retina screens either in self-isolation or among self-selected people pods.

Instead of caps and gowns you've had to wear personal protective equipment (PPE). Instead of receiving your diplomas on a stage before your family and friends, you've been reduced to a Zoom rectangle, YouTube video, or both. You've endured as many indignities as allowable, indeed mandated, by law. You've been deemed more or less too young or unessential, therefore late in getting your vaccinations, if at all. You've been unable to socialize or celebrate with the full cohort of classmates, and you've been inconvenienced by time-zone variations.

Tough luck.

You can take some solace in the realization you're not alone. Everyone is in the same boat—the good ship COVID.

For some it has been a rough voyage. However, for others it's been a smooth cruise. Those who lost loved ones deserve so much more than sympathy. Many who were left unscathed must be grateful for a veritable yearlong holiday.

Okay, the truth is that working remotely, especially for a design student, is no picnic, but for some it's been a kind of free lunch. While many of you have suffered degrees of PTSD, others used the crisis productively to create a slew of entrepreneurial opportunities. The pandemic demanded innovative design practice and strategic thinking more than ever before—whether to create viable lifestyle alternatives or to take the time needed to pursue your expressive ventures.

Some of you engaged in public service while others followed the muse. Rather than limit employment (and despite the high unemployment rates in other industries and crafts) designers were needed to solve new problems and unforeseen necessities. Whether designing a cautionary poster or novel ways to socially commune, designers were called upon to help relieve the bombardment of travails imposed upon us by

COVID-19 and its nasty variants. The pandemic was bad but arguably not the fires of hell. History is replete with worse aberrations.

Then again, look at the upside. Less air, highway, and city traffic equaled less pollution (trees are greener this spring). Wearing face masks reduced the spread of various airborne illnesses (colds were down and flu was negligible). Quarantine gave legitimate excuses for not meeting up with anyone you didn't want to see. You were the master of your own domain (even if it was a cramped dorm room). Stress was distributed in a more equal manner. And "diversity, equality, inclusion" (DEI) was brought to the fore in many institutions where inequality, abuse, and racism had previously been taken for granted.

There were lots of ancillary consequences, both good and bad. With remote classes, students were able to visit guest and expert lectures that would have been impossible otherwise. Streaming films, conferences, and other events were a boon to education and entertainment—sometimes merging the two into a teach-in fiesta. Most of these virtual assets were probably going to happen in the future anyway, but the pandemic sped the deployment of distance classes more quickly.

Many people tragically lost their jobs, incomes, and savings. But where would we have been with considerably less access to products and commodities, without the online retail portals that have been essential to daily existence and, therefore, more profitable than ever? We hope profits will work their way to workers.

Although social distancing prevented in-person family gatherings, holiday celebrations, and collective grieving, exacerbating our loneliness and despair, the pandemic forced all of us to reevaluate what is most valued as human experience.

As the virus danger "recedes," in large part through the concerted efforts of many intelligent people who fought the foe with discipline and courage (despite the stupid political intransience of some), designers, design educators, and design administrators must now learn important lessons to prepare for the future.

Let's recall the story of the "Three Little Pigs" (thanks to Steven Guarnaccia), who each received architectural commissions to build their own houses, all to serve as protection (let's say from swine flu or an impending wolf-borne disease). The tale speaks volumes about the importance of making the right design decisions:

> *The first little pig met a man carrying a bundle of straw.*
> *"Excuse me," said the first little pig politely. "Would you please sell some of your straw so I can make a house?"*
> *The man readily agreed and the first little pig went off to find a good place to build his house.*
> *The other little pigs carried on along the road and, soon, they met a man carrying a bundle of sticks.*
> *"Excuse me," said the little pig politely. "Would you please sell me some sticks so I can build a house?"*
> *The man readily agreed and the little pig said goodbye to his brother.*
> *The third little pig didn't think much of their ideas:*

*"I'm going to build myself a much bigger, better, stronger house," he thought, and he carried off down the road until he met a man with a cartload of bricks.*
*"Excuse me," said the third little pig, as politely as his mother had taught him.*
*"Please can you sell me some bricks so I can build a house?"*
*"Of course," said the man. "Where would you like me to unload them?"*
*The third little pig looked around and saw a nice patch of ground under a tree.*
*"Over there," he pointed.*

They all set to work, and by nighttime the house of straw and the house of sticks were built, but the house of bricks was only just beginning to rise above the ground. The first and second little pigs laughed; they thought their brother was really silly having to work so hard when they had finished.

I think you all know the ending. When designing to prevent catastrophe, think bricks!

# A FOGGY CRYSTAL BALL

E very talk I give to student groups usually ends with basically the same question: "What is the future of graphic design?" Somewhat facetiously but truthfully, I answer: "If I knew, I'd be doing it." In fact, my crystal ball is usually foggy, but I do have a clear idea worth considering. It has nothing to do with the inevitable end of paper or irrepressibility of the World Wide Web or the rise of artificial intelligence. The fact is we're already living in the future, and it is now and it is you. It includes everything we do today and will continue to do tomorrow, with the addition of a few discoveries along the way. That itself is enough, don't you think?

Moreover, you're not really asking me, an aging mortal who used a rotary phone, to be Nostradamus. You want to make certain that there is a job waiting for you—in fact, many jobs—and that you have the talent and skill to be among those who are tapped to do those jobs. Behind every question about the future, is what can I do now? Which makes sense. Many of you probably took on considerable debt to get a design education and you want some assurances that it was not in vain.

I cannot, however, offer that career counseling. Every day you learn more than I know. Still, I can tell you that the future—even as it occurs at today's accelerated speed—doesn't happen overnight. It takes a few days, months, even years. So if you do what you already do well, while keeping your eye on the horizon, you'll figure out the future. That said, thinking ahead is essential to any creative survival. As newly minted graduates, you're too young to get stuck in ruts of convention. But rather than ask me what the future will be, make the future your own.

There are some of you here who will graduate and go on to invent, if you haven't already done so, new ways of conceiving, making, and communicating messages—of becoming form-givers and (in the argot of today) influencers. Graphic designers are at a perfect juncture between old and new technologies to create "products" and involve themselves in "ventures" and start-ups. My concept of the present-future of graphic design has always long been about independent thought leading to autonomous results. This isn't to say that designers will abandon all client-driven work for the sanctity of their own laboratories. It means that my hobby horse is design entrepreneurship and the ABCs of "art, business, culture." Art is inherent in everything a designer does (it might also be called *craft* and can be defined as combining ingenuity with aesthetic quality); business is essential to everything a designer does, especially to be able to sustain the art; and culture is the structure that designers continually build through their wares.

The second question I am most asked by students is what should they do right out of school. Should they go to work for a major or minor corporation or a big or small design firm, be a single proprietor, or start a freelance studio? You don't need a soothsayer for that. Everyone will say do what makes sense. If you want to go into a special area of design, do it! If you want to learn what you missed in school, do it! If you want to experience an experience, do that too! Very few designers are equipped to jump from the cloistered academy into the fire and brimstone of a self-run business. But some are adept and courageous. Do that too!

Whatever the decision, the commencement is a beginning. I suspect that everyone, no matter how accomplished, would like a chance to commence again (I know I do). This is a time to aggressively push forward, try the tried and untried, and show us all why you are the future.

# THE TIME TO INNOVATE

- - - - - - - - - - - - - - - -

**T**his is an amazing and critical time in our history—your history. Creativity is arguably America's number one economic and cultural asset. Conceiving, making, and producing ingenious, indeed extraordinary, ideas are within the hands of the entrepreneurial designer. And they are wanted and needed by the vanguard corporations that value creative outcomes. This is *your* time.

But I'm not here to cheerlead for something that many of you already know . . . and that some of you are already doing. Today I want to take a brief moment to talk about *time*.

All your skill and talent is dependent on how you perceive *time*. Einstein believed that the past, present, and future all exist simultaneously. I wish this were entirely true. I wish we could control time and our place in it.

*/////*

**I**'m no Einstein, but I've been thinking more and more about how our concept of time as either temporal or eternal causes certain problems. Whether we practice a religion or not, time in Judeo-Christian thinking is "the arena of man's decision on his way to an eternal destiny." Time is skewed toward defining the space between a beginning and an end. This suggests a philosophical problem, but maybe it is actually a design problem too, though it is not one easily solved by redesigning a watch face without any numbers. Or, as they do in Las Vegas, eliminate clocks entirely.

Time is our tool, not our master. But as Marshall McLuhan rightly said, "We shape our tools and thereafter our tools shape us." In other words, over time we have become slaves to *time*—and by extension we are burdened by routine.

Time is finite and infinite, *temporal* and *eternal* and neither concept is very comforting. Not having enough time is frustrating, while having *too much* time can be daunting. But time, I recently read, and I love the concept, is only quantitative and not qualitative. What you accomplish in a span of time is not determined by the time you have but by how devoted you are to reaching a goal.

As you begin your creative lives and livelihoods, how you balance, indeed control, time is of the essence. Yet how time manages you is too often what occurs instead in most of our lives. Creative people like you exist in a time paradox.

So many of you believe there is only limited time to make your mark, and yet you also know it takes time to make truly valuable contributions. Creativity is one endeavor, unlike athletics, where time does not diminish capacity.

Yet digital technology has accelerated time and timekeeping. This is another paradox. While it is exciting to be able to produce our work at ever-greater speeds, expectations—our own and our client's—increase as the time for reflection decreases.

Rapid prototyping may be a boon to some industries, but it imposes speed as an ultimate virtue. Believe me, beating the clock does not ensure great work.

Here's a little parable I'd like to share with you: Taking express trains may get you to where you're going faster, but more often than not, too early. And then what? More time to check your email or Twitter feed? Nonetheless, we all wish we had more time . . .

Think about that wonderful Sunday every fall when (if you live on the East Coast of the United States) we move our clocks back one hour. I long for and savor that day, even though I know I pay it forward in the spring.

Since Eastern Standard Time comes only once a year, I have a time-cheating method—call it a time pyramid scheme—that lasts all year. I turn my bedside clock ahead by twenty minutes. I'm sure some of you here must do something like that. Then, owing to some flaw in the machinery, every three days or so, the clock also advances by a minute on its own.

If I had continued my own studies I might be able to do the math. I can tell you that by the end of the month I've accrued a good number of extra minutes, which I use for work or other things. I know I'm stealing from Peter to pay Paul; intellectually I realize free extra time cannot exist. Still the delusion works until the weekend, when I am so tired I can't get out of bed.

At any time, but certainly as you get older, time is the most valuable, yet ethereal thing—you can never, ever possess it. So you have to make the best of it. You have to use it wisely to get everything you can get from it.

Both my parents died recently. They were in their early to mid-nineties. Their time was apparently up. But the time they had was remarkably joyful and productive. When the end comes, however, it seems that the time was too short. Being creative is one way to compensate for this brief stay on earth. And I'm not trying to be maudlin.

For the past three or four years your time has been filled with creative studies. Now comes the time for creative production. You are ready to make things—great things, however you might define what you mean by great. Tomorrow, probably in the late afternoon, when you wake up after your postgraduation partying, your sense of time will be different than it has been up to now. Schooltime and work time are as different as peas and carrots (or gas and electric). Tomorrow, the clock begins to tick off the rest of your life.

So, use this time to make your time valuable. More importantly, define what time means for you. It does not have to be a conventional definition. And it should not be based on a routine timesheet.

Einstein proved that time is relative, not absolute as Newton claimed. You can design your time for optimum impact on you and others.

I'd want to end by paraphrasing the great British philosopher Sir Michael Philip (Mick) Jagger:

Time, time, time is on your side, yes it is.

So, congratulations to all of you graduating in the class of 2013. And thank you, College for Creative Studies, for validating my time card.

# QUESTIONS FOR BUDDING DESIGNERS

- - - - - - - - - - - - - - - - - - - -

**T**he blooming of multicolored academic robes—a chromatic bouquet of academic regalia—means just one thing: It is spring commencement season. That joyful time for students who are ready to join the world's design fields. Bravo! But for me it means anticipating the call that never comes. I'm talking about a request inviting me to offer ten to fifteen minutes of wisdom to a cohort of newly graduated artists and designers. This spring is no exception. However, adhering to tradition, I write a commencement address just in case a scheduled speaker gets ill, tests positive, or misses their plane. This year's topic is not, however, my usual optimistic hurrah but rather some important questions that many of you who will have to address at some time during your professional lives, particularly now that we've entered an age of increased (and not altogether unwarranted) sensitivity. I admit up front that I do not have answers but knowing the questions is a good beginning. So, let's begin . . .

What do you say (or not) when you don't like someone's work?

Should you volunteer an opinion if you think someone's work is not to your taste?

How honest should you be with a colleague? Underling? Student? Stranger? Is honest criticism abusive?

Can harsh criticism be construed as abusive?

What is more important, the quality of work? Or the feelings of the worker?

How do you balance the two?

You are working with someone who oversteps their job description. How do you respond?

If that person is threatening your position, how do you respond?

How do you address (or not) professional jealousy in the workplace?

If a colleague gets promoted and is now your superior, what is your response?

If you do not like a fellow worker, what do you say or how do you act?

If you are displeased with a client, what do you do?

How do you handle conflict with a professional friend?

Can respect overcome animosity?

If you believe your personal and/or professional ethics have been compromised, what do you do?

With colleagues, clients, students, or superiors, how do you balance differences in political, religious, and philosophical beliefs?

At what point do you act upon any of these issues?

Should you seek out professional guidance if any of these issues arise?

Here are some examples that have worked for me:

*What do you say (or not) when you don't like someone's work?*

If you are asked for a critique, honesty is best. But someone once told me to look at the best part of someone's work. With a portfolio, for instance, instead of a blanket rejection, I single out the one or two examples that should be the high bar, explain why that is the case, and that should be the goal. That avoids saying that everything is bad. But what if everything is below "my standard"? There are two alternatives. One is easy to say: "This approach does not appeal to my subjective taste" puts the onus on me (which may be the reality anyway). The other is hard: Unvarnished truth. Whatever that may be, like "You don't have the skill" or "This is a competitive field and you need to invest more time and effort to make the cut." Within those poles there is a lot that can be improvised.

*Should you volunteer an opinion if you think your response to someone's work is not to your taste?*

Volunteering is tricky. Often someone will show work simply to show the work. They may, in fact, be quite proud of it. Or maybe they are insecure and afraid to ask for an opinion. The best option is to take the temperature of the presenter. Silence says a lot. Saying "interesting but I'm not sure it works" is my usual noncommittal response, which leaves the door open for a follow-up question. The most radical, and possibly helpful, response is complete candor.

*How honest should you be with a colleague? Underling? Student? Stranger?*

Honesty may not be appreciated at the moment it is given. Or it may be just what is needed. With an underling or student, total honesty is the only correct response. An employee must meet your standard, A student comes to you to learn. A stranger? Again, it depends on what you are willing to invest, but dishonesty isn't worth your time.

I hope this was useful for some. Now, go out and start working.

# COMPETENCY IS NOT AN END PRODUCT

I retired almost ten years ago from my job at the *New York Times* and left behind my private office, comfy chair, computer, and almost all of my computer design skills. While I was the art director of the *Book Review* for almost three decades, I needed to learn various new methods and technologies—from how to prepare images for the engraver when we printed on letterpress; how to use a user-unfriendly Harris terminal when we switched over to photo type; preparing page comps on the early Apples and Macs using Quark, then switching over to InDesign (and assorted upgrades); and building press-ready pages populated with text, Photoshop, and Illustrator files. I retained the rote basics—enough to get me through the day—but never mastered advanced techniques (like linking text to image, style sheets, and other now-routine stuff). Still, I was competent.

However, when I returned my ID card to HR, my procedural memory was wiped clean too. The erasure was so sudden that the famed neurologist Dr. Oliver Sacks could have used me as a case study.

I once knew a guy who had suffered a temporary paralyzing stroke. After six months in therapy, he relearned how to use his motor skills. He was fine. Then one day he decided to play tennis. It was his first time on the court since the stroke, and he was volleying very well, yet slowly. Then his opponent returned a serve that went over my friend's head. He froze, unable to move backward. His opponent, who had some therapeutic knowledge, jumped over the net and went to my friend's aid.

Apparently, during therapy, my friend was not taught to move in reverse—he simply did not know how to walk backward. This condition, called "learned nonuse," causes the brain to have even more difficulty paying attention to stroke-affected muscles, therefore making it harder to rehabilitate these muscles and over-relying on unaffected parts of the body. This is where the phrase "use it or lose it!" comes from. My friend's tennis opponent actually taught him to walk backward then and there.

"Use it or lose it" in my case is presumably solvable. I use a computer every day for writing in Word (an old version), Zoom (which I regularly update), FaceTime, building Keynotes, opening PDFs, searching with Google, and other simple things. I can open a file in Photoshop and do rudimentary tasks, but, frankly, that's not enough to fulfill my needs or expectations. Even with cheat sheets I have problems following procedures. In effect, I have become incompetent. So, when it comes to making my ideas come to life onscreen, including animations, GIFs, and whatever, I have to have someone do it for me.

At first, I thought that this is part of the aging adventure. There is only so much bandwidth in the brain and since I do not have to regularly design or make files for a book, magazine, or poster, I just pass it on to someone who will follow my direction (or do something better). During this pandemic season, it is no longer a viable solution. It is lazy. However, starting from scratch is not an option.

Fran Lebowitz admitted on her Netflix special *Pretend It's a City* miniseries directed by Martin Scorsese that she did not have any marketable skills—she was *useless* for anything but driving a cab (which she did for a year) or waiting on tables (which was iffy when years ago she did it). Lebowitz does not own a computer or smartphone or have an email account. At least I have all. She also suffers from years of "writer's blockade." Her "active compensatory factor" is a bitingly hilarious wit. So, she can make a good living through her talent for talk on the speaking circuit. But the pandemic has been a disaster. I sympathize, but eccentricity only goes so far.

Yet look who's talking. Being unable to do all but the simplest design tasks, I am forced to do dumb work-arounds. Instead of learning the latest version of InDesign, I screw around with Word (I literally cut and paste, then scan and make a PDF). Without knowledge of Photoshop or Illustrator, I make Keynote slides (make screenshots, cut and paste, make JPEGs, etc.)—I can cope by stitching things together. Usually, I just write down what I'm trying to do and hope that someone with skill (and talent) is not busy or takes pity. It is not ideal, but in lieu of reprogramming, it is a plan.

It is a true fact that once you learn how to swim or ride a bicycle you never forget. It must be true. I have not been on a bike for decades and the other day I hopped on one and within seconds was riding without holding the handlebars (swimming is another thing altogether). Why is this so? Because the action gets stored within the procedural memory, which governs the use of objects and movements. I wish procedural memory could work for me with digital design tools. No such luck.

# SELF-ANALYSIS BABBLE

'␣ve been spending a lot of time neurotically reevaluating my life. An overdue existential reckoning-self-indulgent-anxiety-provoking-stress-triggering-late-life-whiling-away-of-the-pre-post-pandemic-aftermath.

One of the mind games I've considered is (and I'll wager that most of you have asked yourselves already) why after all the years of being in and around the business of commercial art, graphic design, illustration, propaganda and punditry, I signed up in the first place? Was it really a consuming passion to make creative things and ultimately earn accolades as a result? Or what?

When I was five to seven years old I desperately wanted to be an actor doing commercials, game shows, plays, and whatever would put me in the limelight. Many classmates had the same ambitions (or their parents did) and some seemed to flourish doing so (for a while, at least, until they got into their tweens and could no longer get roles). But, for me, after two years of open and closed auditions (and having to dye my hair blond, which was a necessity for black-and-white TV work), I reluctantly accepted I was not destined for even walk-on parts (though I did have one).

So I pivoted. Instead of acting, I glommed on to the idea I'd become a satirist!

My Uncle Walter was a professor of American history at Columbia University. I learned to love topical satire from listening to his LPs of routines by Lenny Bruce, Mort Sahl, Stan Freiberg, Nichols and May, and Bob and Ray. Brilliant all! He introduced me to cartoonists: Jules Feiffer and Walt Kelly were comics heroes. But forever my favorite "textbook" on the practice and joy of great satire was *MAD Magazine*.

Digging through my memory chests, I found a cache of early *MAD* paperback anthologies from the late fifties and early sixties—most from Harvey (the) Kurtzman's great epoch (featuring the artists Will [the] Elder and Wally [the] Wood).

As I kid, I'd collect deposits from bottles and cans thrown willy-nilly in the abundant vacant lots, where I summered in Long Beach, Long Island, during the late fifties and early sixties; when I had scrounged enough coins, I'd run down to the Cozy Nook luncheonette and buy the latest offerings off the paperback rack (and an Orange Crush). The cheap newsprint pages are now ragged, torn, moldy, and yellow. Treasures!

I've kept them for decades because this is why I originally wished I was in the business we dispassionately now call "VizCom" or whatever other abbrev is shorthand for what we do.

I didn't get into it just to make lovely typography (I didn't even know what typography was in my eights and tens) or design handsome pages for books and magazines, although I greatly admire the folk that do. But my gut passion and need has always been to conceive clever ideas that would make readers think, and even more important, through words and pictures, images that would make them laugh. Hearing a full-throated, honest belly laugh, not just a pleasant polite chuckle, is the best feeling in the world.

*MAD Magazine*, especially the early years, gave that brain-to-belly stuff to me in spades, diamonds, hearts, and clubs. As I reacquainted myself with the few pages I salvaged, I am again reminded what I never entirely achieved and why I entered into this business in other roles as a consequence. I'm not unhappy, but wish I had the ability to do what the old gang at *MAD* did. Too bad there ain't no original *MAD* no more.

*MAD* was glorious Madness! Sublime Madness! Pure Madness!

# WHY I TEACH, WHAT I TEACH

- - - - - - - - - - - - - - - - - - - - - - -

To answer the question "why I teach," I must return to why I design, why I art direct, why I write, and why I helped found the MFA Design Criticism program, which morphed into this one. It's a simple evolution.

I stumbled into graphic design while pursuing a job as a cartoonist and illustrator for an underground newspaper. I loved to draw, although not very well. My favorite pastime was autobiographical cartoons in the manner of Jules Feiffer; at sixteen years old my ambition was to get them published, but every magazine I pestered turned me down. I was given a job doing mechanicals at one of them, however, when I was seventeen, where by chance the editor liked and published the cartoons. Eventually, I realized my drawing skill was severely limited and I devoted myself to learning (on my own) typography and page layout. This helped to push me up the ladder to art direction. After a few years, I was hired as art director of the *New York Times* op-ed page. There, I hired great illustrators (old vets and newcomers) to do work and conceive ideas that I was incapable of doing myself, but rather felt comfortable critiquing their work. ("Those who can't do, teach; those who can't teach, teach gym"—Woody Allen.) Understanding my limitations in that role, I became obsessively interested in the history of caricature and illustration. I curated exhibits and wrote a few articles and conducted oral history interviews. I liked the writing process, even though I had no real idea what I was doing. I also enjoyed the research—finding artifacts from the past that prefigured the present art. I began to write about this history (the truth is, if I could have stayed in college, I would have majored in American history). I used graphic art as a lens through which I explored political and social history.

Did I mention I was born, more or less, into a left-liberal family with an uncle who taught history at Columbia? I was raised in the mid-1960s to be left-leaning in New York. So my natural inclination was to study, practice, and embrace politics—especially politics in graphic arts. To this day I am amazed that I somehow parlayed these interests and skills into a job writing about graphic design, illustration, satiric art and popular culture. There were not many people doing what I was doing when I started doing it. Now it is an academic discipline.

I was asked to teach at SVA in the newly formed MFA Illustration as Visual Journalism department. I taught illustration history. I also began writing about it for *PRINT* magazine, *GRAPHIS* and even the *New York Times* (where I was an art director of the *Book Review* section for thirty years). Twenty years ago, I was asked to conceive an MFA Design program—the first in SVA's history. It was called the MFA

**FOR THE LOVE OF DESIGN**

Design: Designer As Author. By author, my cofounder Lita Talarico and I really meant "entrepreneur." But at the same time there was movement and growth in design writing and research. I edited the *AIGA Journal* for eleven years and started writing books too. I believed there was a need for designers to write their own history and criticism, that writing was an essential skill. The legendary designer Massimo Vignelli said in a speech that "Design will never be considered a real profession without a body of criticism." I took that literally and instituted a critical column for *PRINT* magazine, wrote critically for others and convinced SVA's president, David Rhodes, that it would be a useful master's program.

When together with Alice Twemlow we founded DCrit (her coinage), I requested a spot teaching a research and writing class devoted to telling the stories about designed objects—and since most everything is designed (good or bad) it made sense. The conceit, however, was it would be the "no-Google class." Students were prohibited from doing their research with Google. The students thought it sadistic, but they, in fact, understood that without the help of Google they needed to dig into the weeds, go to the library, follow leads, and develop research methodologies. Guest writers, editors, collectors, curators, librarians, and others were invited to explain their procedures and, in the end, papers were written about a wide range of physical and virtual objects. It proved very satisfying for all of us.

When the one-year MA was introduced, the class was shaved down from fifteen to five weeks. For two years I eliminated the no-Google component. Times do change, and Google was then more important, at least for data-based research and factual confirmation, than before. This past year I reinstituted a no-Google segment of the class, sending the students to libraries and to do interviews with primary sources. I haven't lost my excitement when it comes time to read and hear (since they must make verbal presentations) what the students discover and, as important, how they turn their facts into engaging storytelling.

Why do I teach? I love to learn.

# INSOMNIA: A WAKE-UP CALL

**"T**he best cure for insomnia is to get a lot of sleep," my primary care physician told me during our last Zoom call. It wasn't funny then or the half dozen other times he's delivered that line since I began experiencing chronic sleep deprivation.

**I couldn't sleep a wink!** Tossing and turning, crawling in and out of bed, getting increasingly agitated with each amplified tick of the clock across from the bed. My head fills with gobs of minutiae, like the fact that my doctor's medical wisdom is not fully covered by insurance, and other tidbits run on a loop in my brain. But I know using this as an excuse avoids the real reasons for my sleep deprivation. At my ripe age, there are more, not less, things to worry about, and getting requisite sleep is extremely difficult.

**My pillow at 11:00 p.m.!** By 2:45 a.m. I realize I will never sleep again as the multitude of things seep into my porous skull—worrisome things, bothersome things, and unimportant things, like what to have for breakfast. Still awake at 4:15 a.m., I know that if I do not get at least a few hours of shut-eye, I'll be nodding off at the computer, struggling not to close my heavy eyelids during the day's interminable Zoom meetings.

**Zoom sleep!** I thought I had tricks to avoid embarrassment—like, if I keep the lights low, no one can see me dozing. "Can you see it when my lids are closing?" I sometimes ask my closest coworker. "Sure, I do," she responds. "That's why periodically I ask you questions, to give you a virtual nudge."

**Take meds!** For two years I've experienced three to four nights when despite ingesting 3 grams of melatonin each night—and although my body is kaput—it is impossible to shut off my mind. During the day I am likely to drift off at any moment. Yet the minute the clock hits 11 p.m.—time for bed—every infinitesimal meaningful or meaningless thought collides into a massive ball. When it does, I ask myself "Should I write some of these thoughts down?" I figure that the time should not go entirely to waste. But I don't. I just think more about stuff—good, bad, and easily forgotten stuff. The stream ebbs and flows, but it won't stop until the alarm rings.

**Triggering insomnia!** In my case it started one night, when I happily anticipated seeing a finished copy of a book I'd worked on, that was being delivered the next day. Spending the bedtime hours imagining turning the pages over and over made sleep impossible and began a habit that continues today.

**Sleep is perplexing!** As a kid I used to wonder how could I just close my eyes and—bingo—be transported to places so real yet incongruous and filled with alternate doses of terror and pleasantness. Where did these images come from? I looked forward to the dream state as a vacation from reality. Then, somewhere I took a wrong turn and got on the sour milk train moving further and further, deeper and deeper to places unknown and unpleasant when the dream of reason created monsters. Recently I've been at the point where trying to restfully sleep has become a chore at best and impossibility at worse.

**Suffering!** I presume everyone (if anyone is) reading this has suffered insomnia triggered by work, personal, social, asocial, or political anxiety. Maybe a proportion of you suffer from the hallucinogenic aftermath too, a kind of narcolepsy. If you are struggling, unable to alleviate or reduce your predisposition to insomnia, my heart goes out to you.

**Answers!** When he's not telling jokes, my doctor suggests that two hours before bedtime I turn off all screens—TVs, iPhones, laptops, iPads—anything that emits other than normal, incandescent light. He recommends light (no pun intended) reading to help slow down the mind. I comply—most of the time. The exception is when I am excitedly writing or researching for an article, I can't just put on the brakes when the process is going well. Stopping just forces me to continue thinking about the next sentence and paragraph. Sometimes, I'll discover a point that I had missed, or an otherwise elusive ending. Endings are always hard; it is a sin to lose the train of thought.

**Training!** My choice is to either get off the train or stay aboard, throw caution to the wind, turn on the screen to low light, and continue to write. I am convinced that once I get the idea out of my head, I am freer to fall asleep. Of course, it never works exactly as planned.

**My fallback?** I always have a book to read. But what kind? I am told that most of my favorite books about war, politics, and history are not suitable for bedtime. But if I try to read them a few hours before bedtime, I invariably fall asleep for an hour or so, then wake up startled and find it impossible to get back to sleep again. Do you see my predicament?

**The garbage trucks!** I live in a neighborhood where private carters illegally pick up industrial-strength trash (i.e., large, heavy metallic objects) at 11:00 p.m., 2:00 a.m. and 4:00 a.m. (they must stop from 10:00 p.m. to 6:00 a.m.). Even after scores of complaints to the community board and police station right next door to my building, I still can set a watch by the truck noise. I don't wear a watch, and I cannot see the clock without my glasses, but on those rare nights when I'm not sound asleep, I hear them, at their appointed times. Although the garbage truck noise saves me the effort of putting on my glasses, once I am awakened, I do not have a prayer of going back to sleep while compactors are clanging and engines are whirring.

**City windows!** A triple-pane window with heavy soundproof glass in each frame prevents the majority of ambient street noise. Without them, life in my building would be unbearable. But this soundproofing does not squelch the garbage trucks and blaring fire engine sirens. (Did I mention that fire trucks from the station one block north use my street when they speed eastward?)

 *In* **words!** So many words with the prefix "in" have such terrible meanings—insane, insecure, incontinent, indictable, incapable, inexcusable. Inconsequential? Maybe! But it is just one of the scores of things that run through my head when I should be peacefully asleep *in* bed.

# ON BEING A DISPLACED PERSON

I feel sad for people who do not have offices. It is not that those who have them are smarter than those who do not, but there is a difference between having a room to work in, large or small, with a window or without, which is an extension of an aspect of their personality. My office is definitely me. Even amid the extreme clutter in mine, I take pride in my office filled with art and artifacts that officially define who I am and what I do. Since the COVID-19 shutdown on March 13, 2020, I have been forbidden by my doctors from using my office.

I have become a displaced person.

The other day, after hearing the news that a second lockdown was imminent, I walked to my office building and stood outside for about fifteen minutes, looking up, assessing the risks at this time. I knew that only one other colleague would be in the studio and I could doubtless social distance. My intent was to sign in, take an empty elevator (although it had been occupied before I entered), follow the stringent safety protocols, and stay at my desk only long enough to gather a few necessary items. I determined the odds were in my favor of a brief visit.

After considering the options (and ultimate necessity), I couldn't abide being so close, yet so far. I took the plunge. And what an uneasy feeling it was.

It did not help that I had just finished reading *Earth Abides* by George R. Stewart, a 1949 novel about most of the world's human population being decimated by an unknown and incurable virus. It was a bad idea to read it in the first place but I thought I could handle it. The setting is outside Los Angeles in a small community of survivors that takes place over the course of fifty years since the Great Disaster. This mysterious apocalypse is followed over time by infestations of ants, rats, locusts, rattlesnakes, fires, and other uncontrollable ruin to the infrastructure, including loss of electricity, water supply, and other necessities. It traces the life of "Ish" (Isherwood), who eventually meets other vagabond survivors, some of whom mate, spawn children, and form the Tribe as a means to rebuild, indeed start a new civilized existence. I admit that watching the new Borat movie was less depressing in one way though more wincing in others, but *Earth Abides* was craftily constructed in terms of the evolution of the characters and setting. I wanted to stop, however, at given points but stuck with it if only to learn the fates of all concerned. (No spoiler alert from me.)

Entering my office for the first time since March, I felt a twinge of what Ish might have experienced after returning to his California birthplace a few years after the Great Disaster and finding it just as his parents had left it. Everything was the same but nonetheless different. It was extremely messy since I did not consider that I would not return within a few weeks (the lockdown for me lasted thirteen weeks until moving upstate for another three months). What's more I'm messy. It was also sanitarily clean, because the cleaning staff was given access on a regular basis. It was filled with unopened piles of mail because I get lots of letters, zines, and boxes. It was disconcertingly weird.

My stuff was there but I was not. I was an interloper. It was like visiting a re-creation, frozen in time, like W. A. Dwiggins's studio at the Boston Public Library or Theodore Roosevelt's bedroom in his birthplace brownstone on 20th Street (only a few avenues away) or the bedroom of Edwin Booth (brother of John Wilkes Booth) preserved at the Players club at Gramercy Park. I was displaced.

To be clear, I was not a displaced person in the same way that devastated refugees from war or natural calamity are who lost all their properties, homes, countries and families—I still have a home, family, friends, and possessions. If I choose to break my doctor's rules, I can risk returning. But the sensation of being displaced from who I am and the rupture from what I do was profound. I had enough time to retrieve two random items from the many, before in my mind's eye I imagined those microscopic, eerie little COVID-19 plush viruses massing to attack. I guess from now on I'll wait until the war is finally won before I return.

PART 2
policies

# PART 2:
# POLITICS

# WAR! WHAT IS IT GOOD FOR?

**D**o not be surprised by how much warfare has actually contributed to our world. From devastating destruction has arisen new machines, technologies, communications, and culture, some of it best left on the battlefield to rot and others not. In her excellent new history *War: How Conflict Shaped Us*, Margaret MacMillan, emeritus professor of international history at the University of Oxford and professor at the University of Toronto, examines how wars have been the violent means of acquiring power and property and protecting them too, how language and behavior have been greatly shaped by war, and how war appears to be a virus which has no cure, just lulls and Pax periods. Although this is not a design book, so many consequences of wars, including innovations through design, have emerged. The definition of war is diplomacy gone (by other means) awry; but war is also a laboratory for everything from foods and medicines to clothing, from weapons to methods of controlling thought through propaganda.

Professor MacMillan's exhaustive research into a broad span of war covers the Greek and Roman phalanx (a grid of men in battle), to the ritual of armies meeting for only one day on a battlefield for a circumscribed time frame and then after a decisive battle determining a winner—not unlike a football or chess match—to computerized, arcade-like current wars using drones to pinpoint targets. It is disheartening to realize (especially during the rise in armed militias) that *tactics* and *strategy*, among other concepts derived through warfare, are used to describe branding and advertising *campaigns*. In fact, war is a basis for discussions about today's design theory and practice. If you attend any branding lecture, seminar, or conference, it is likely that military principles will be embedded in the vocabulary of the rhetoric. Even the word "freelance" comes from "free lance," a mercenary or soldier of fortune.

One chapter in particular, "War in Our Imaginations and Our Memories," addresses the impact on art and design and vice versa. Modern war, for instance, created a need for a new visual and oral language to describe the unspeakable industrial carnage. "Plays, poems, novels, paintings, sculpture, photographs, music and films," writes MacMillan, "shape how we—warriors and civilians alike—imagine and think about war" and that can trigger many feelings from "the heroic and glorious to the cruelty and horror."

War is a double-edged sword for many artists and designers—for those who abhor and support—forcing them to experiment with ways of achieving emotional unvarnished and patriotic idealized depictions. Glorifying and condemning war often rely on the same visual images, only presented in different contexts. World War I proved that the same celebratory commemorations as in eighteenth- and nineteenth-century visuals no longer held sway. MacMillan, quoting a 1916 cultural review, says "No artist can give us a total impression of the things that go on in night and fog, under earth and above the clouds. . . . The death-defying men who march past and pounce on the enemy in battlefield canvases of the old school have disappeared. In place were introduced images of terror that showed the physical cost of war. MacMillan quotes the Swiss painter Félix Vallotton, who was one of the most strident graphic commentators for the French satiric journal *L'Assiette au Beurre*: "From now on I no longer believe in blood-soaked sketches, in realistic painting, in things seen, or even experienced. It is mediation alone which can draw out the essential synthesis of such evocation." This is borne out in his painting *Verdun*, one of the bloodiest battles, which mutilated the men of the French and German armies.

Once war, notably in the West, was considered an honorable obligation, an oath-based responsibility to fight and die for monarch or deity and land. Twentieth-century war was no longer the same kind of game with gentleman's rules and wartime etiquette. Among the best parts of this absorbing book (again, whether or not it is read as a design text) is MacMillan's writing on the avant-garde modern artist/designers who are the foundation of the Eurocentric canon. I quote a portion of a paragraph here:

> Perhaps it was merely a coincidence that in different cities across Europe and in the New World artists were experimenting before 1914 with forms that suited the battlefields to come. The Cubists were developing a new idiom to capture the fragmentation of the world around them, while the Futurists tried to find ways to paint movement itself. In England, Vorticists wanted to smash the existing order to pieces and that, for them, meant a new geometric style that reflected the jagged nature of the world. Which, it turned out represented the chaos of the battlefields covered with barbed wire, rocket bursts and waves of gas.

To end on a definitive note that contradicts MacMillan's superb scholarship, here Edwin Starr's 1970 lyric says it all:

> *War, huh . . .*
> *What is it good for?*
> *Alright, absolutely nothing . . .*
> *War!*

# TO FREE OR NOT TO FREE?

- - - - - - - - - - - - - - - - - -

**A**re there limits to free speech? The old canard about not yelling "fire" in a crowded theater is easy to understand. Irresponsible speech, hate speech, libelous speech—indeed, lies of any kind—are not considered free but harmful and often illegal. Yet publicizing unproven, questionable, and contentious theories and rhetoric born of religion, politics, art, and culture that distorts fact is protected under law and can be a dangerous weapon for and against truth. I cannot speak to the legal intricacies of free-speech guidelines, but I am an advocate of free speech principles. I believe that so-called acceptable speech changes as mores progress (or regress). Still, I have biases that can (and do) sometimes override these principles. I cherish liberal interpretations of the rights of free speech. I also have strong ambivalences when some of those biases play out in real time. I guess we all do.

I oppose speech that puts others at risk. Language that agitates for violence and hatred cannot be tolerated and neither should be talk or innuendo that libels and defames. Free speech should not abridge the rights of others to be free. However, this is not absolute. Freedom comes with certain subjective baggage and exacts a moral price.

So, when I saw a protest poster against extraditing Julian Assange to the United States, I had grave misgivings not about hanging it but what it suggests. The idea behind WikiLeaks, to expose restricted information that the public nonetheless has a right to know and, given the wont of government and corporations to keep secrets, is valid. Whistleblowers and leakers have done great service over the span of history, and many of them have suffered severe consequences for their bravery. But motive is a consideration when it is done to damage rather than repair. Leaks must not simply expose wrongdoing but help legally remedy the wrong (if possible). I cannot help but question Assange's motives and reconsider my own support of his reasons for disruption. I support activist disruption when it serves my beliefs (admittedly, I am less of an advocate when it does not). Fighting against injustice is justified. But accepting free speech means understanding its ramifications.

This is where propaganda plays a role. The barrage of propaganda against Assange has raised serious doubts about his veracity. Is his activism for the right or the wrong reasons? Is he protected in the name of journalism, or should he be investigated for political partisanship? This poster makes it seem that America as a nation is against Assange, and that gives me pause. The gag is a clichéd graphic idea and has been used in many different iterations. Is the government trying to gag him? Yes. Do the people feel the same way? Not sure. But that's the responsibility of Americans to determine on their own and not take the propaganda at face value. George Orwell said that if free speech (or liberty) "means anything at all it means the right to tell people what they do not want to hear."

Free speech is not always righteous speech. During the Weimar Republic, Hitler was allowed to freely render his venomous rhetoric, then after it turned violent he was prohibited from public speaking by law. These rights were quickly reinstated by decree—look at how that all turned out. In times of war, information is closely guarded, so it requires strict classification—loose lips do indeed sink ships. Yet "top secret" should not be an excuse for unbridled censorship. Free speech is often used wrongly. That's the gamble. But then again, some speech should be proscribed. Remember we also have the right to remain silent—determining when is the challenge.

# THE PRICE OF FREE SPEECH AND DESIGN

I have been asked to be an "expert" witness in several lawsuits dealing with design and illustration appropriation and plagiarism. I've routinely declined (except once where the evidence was unambiguously egregious) on the grounds that usually I can see from where the contentious work *really* originated. Recently, I was requested via email to include my name on a friend-of-the-court brief in a "freedom of speech" First Amendment case now pending before the United States Supreme Court. The brief, I was told, is intended to clarify for the Court the status of website designers as uniquely creative artists protected by the First Amendment. The ruling, I was told, may ultimately have a long-term impact for other designers. The request was certainly intriguing.

I subscribe to the First Amendment and its protections that are hardwired into contemporary American life. And although I was told that the amicus curiae did not take one side or the other, before committing to signing I did due diligence and asked two "experts" to explain the issues. The experts were circumspect, providing facts without prejudice. After processing what I learned, I felt stuck in a difficult philosophical, ethical, and moral position that pitted my allegiance to the Constitution against my belief in equity and equality. I will try to explain.

But first, a pro forma disclaimer at foot of the email prevents me from quoting from the letter. The case in question, however, is detailed on a number of legal and informational websites including National Association of Attorneys General, Wikipedia and Oyez (the last calls itself "a multimedia archive devoted to making the Supreme Court of the United States accessible to everyone"). Based on what I read about the case, I decided not to give my support, because I felt its intent was ultimately discriminatory.

This case centered on a declaration on the "about" section of the website of a Colorado-based designer's business whose services include the customized design of marriage websites. The principal owner and sole designer is denying services to same-sex marriage/LGBTQ+ customers, a policy based on personal religious belief that objects to and ignores that same-sex marriage was legally upheld by the Supreme Court in June 2015. This case is reminiscent of the narrow 2018 Supreme Court ruling in favor of Masterpiece Cakeshop bakery owner Jack Phillips who refused to make a wedding cake for a same-sex couple also owing to the shop owner's religious convictions. The decision opened a trap door for the litigation of civil versus religious rights. The case I was asked to support has similar implications. The following language from the Oyez site summarizes the case:

Lorie Smith is the owner and founder of a graphic design firm, 303 Creative LLC. She wants to expand her business to include wedding websites. However, she opposes same-sex marriage on religious grounds so she does not want to design websites for same-sex weddings. She wants to post a message on her own website explaining her religious objections to same-sex weddings.

The Colorado Anti-Discrimination Act (CADA) prohibits businesses that are open to the public from discriminating on the basis of numerous characteristics, including sexual orientation. The law defines discrimination not only as refusing to provide goods or services, but also publishing any communication that says or implies that an individual's patronage is unwelcome because of a protected characteristic.

Even before the state sought to enforce CADA against her, Smith and her company challenged the law in federal court, alleging numerous constitutional violations. The district court granted summary judgment for the state, and the US Court of Appeals for the Tenth Circuit affirmed.

On 303 Creative's website one finds a meticulously worded personal statement that reads as follows:

As a Christian who believes that God gave me the creative gifts that are expressed through this business, I have always strived to honor Him in how I operate it. My primary objective is to design and create expressive content— script, graphics, websites, and other creative content—to convey the most compelling and effective message I can to promote my client's purposes, goals, services, products, events, causes, or values. Because of my faith, however, I am selective about the messages that I create or promote—while I will serve anyone I am always careful to avoid communicating ideas or messages, or promoting events, products, services, or organizations, that are inconsistent with my religious beliefs.

Oyez asks: "Does application of the Colorado Anti-Discrimination Act to compel an artist to speak or stay silent violate the Free Speech Clause of the First Amendment?"

The case is now being deliberated by the majority conservative Court.

The question that weighs on me as an individual is: Where do the doctrines of free speech and religious belief conflict with and even abridge the rights of those also entitled to First Amendment protections? The issues are complex but not that difficult to sort out. Religious freedom has long held sway over our secular nation. Laws exist ideally to mete out justice for the greater good but not at the expense of the individual's rights. However, there are work arounds.

The underpinning of the case is the concept that "artistic expression" is a type of speech protected under the First Amendment. Generally, federal, state, and local governments cannot restrict artistic expression based on its message, ideas, subject matter, or content. Yet federal, state, and local governments do often nonetheless impose limitations on artistic expression.

Hence, another dog in the fight is *what is artistic expression?* Is there a distinction between expressionist art and graphic, web design, editorial, or advertising illustration (a.k.a. commercial art)? Are designers considered artists driven by a muse or service providers hired by clients? Is a designer legally obliged to accept all customers? Or at least offer their services to everyone based on the acceptance of reasonable and contractual business practices, such as acceptance of fees and deadlines?

Decades ago, I was denied typesetting services from a type house because the manager objected to the message I was setting with his type. Ad hoc censorship should be difficult to justify today, but in the current climate, who knows.

Colorado's public accommodation clause requires that a "public facing" business provide services to anyone who requests them. This is the legal language (note that "accommodation" means any entity that is open to the public for business):

> (2) (a) It is a discriminatory practice and unlawful for a person, directly or indirectly, to refuse, withhold from, or deny to an individual or a group, because of disability, race, creed, color, sex, sexual orientation, marital status, national origin, or ancestry, the full and equal enjoyment of the goods, services, facilities, privileges, advantages, or accommodations of a place of public accommodation or, directly or indirectly, to publish, circulate, issue, display, post, or mail any written, electronic, or printed communication, notice, or advertisement that indicates that the full and equal enjoyment of the goods, services, facilities, privileges, advantages, or accommodations of a place of public accommodation will be refused, withheld from, or denied an individual or that an individual's patronage or presence at a place of public accommodation is unwelcome, objectionable, unacceptable, or undesirable because of disability, race, creed, color, sex, sexual orientation, marital status, national origin, or ancestry.

On 303's "public facing" website, the designer implies unwillingness to provide services for same-sex marriages, and although it violates Colorado's public accommodation clause, the designer argues her product is artistic expression and, therefore, viable as free speech. So the case before the Supreme Court is "Whether applying a public-accommodation law to compel an artist to speak or stay silent violates the Free Speech Clause of the First Amendment?"

I don't know of a legal statute that definitively states that design is art (only an anecdotal sense and an ethical response): Art is subjective (anyone can call themselves an artist) but whether something is art or not, I do have a gut response to this case: Not all speech is equal. Hate speech, for example, is speech that causes harm or humiliation and is discriminatory. Discrimination is, furthermore, unlawful. While no designer is compelled to take on any (not critical to saving a life) work they do not want to do, there are many legitimate reasons (and also consequences) for not accepting a job. This case may hinge on some legal technicality, but we all must keep this in mind: Whatever the legal outcome of this case, the inalienable right of free speech should in the end not protect beliefs or doctrines that hurt, harm, or humiliate others—and that includes LGBTQ+ partners who are exercising their freedoms too: Life, liberty and the pursuit of happiness through marriage rituals and ceremonies.

# DISSENT AND ADVOCACY

- - - - - - - - - - - - - - - - - - - - - - - - - -

**C**lashes over the limits of academic freedom and political correctness in the educational sphere have triggered generational debates. Is unconditional free speech guaranteed on campus? And what is the definition of free speech? The American historian Richard Hofstader and my uncle, Walter P. Metzger, traced this essential liberty in 1955 in *The Development of Academic Freedom in the United States.* In 1956 Henry Veatch wrote in his review of the book in the *Indiana Magazine of History:*

> Unfortunately, at the present time academic freedom would appear to be one of the poor relations among the various freedoms. For so far as the general public is concerned, any such thing as a claim to academic freedom leaves most people indifferent or, if not indifferent, then mistrustful or even hostile. Worse still, the indifference or mistrust or hostility seems to be compounded of serious misconceptions and misinformation about the nature and purpose of academic freedom.

These issues continue to arise in the academic environment, particularly as relates to the current expressions of dissent and advocacy. I recently became aware of a debate at East Stroudsburg University (ESU) regarding its "Inclusion Project," which included thirty posters. The project was led by art and design professor David Mazure and philosophy Professor T. Storm Heter's Human Rights and Freedom class.

Laura Null on the ESU campus news site reported that the posters were hung throughout the campus, displaying various projects on political, racial/ethical, cultural, and gender differences and barriers and multiple other topics and issues people face every day, with a public forum held to "discuss these posters and allow for the university to give their explanation of the project." Out of these thirty posters, two were most discussed. One featured Martin Luther King Jr. standing in front of a crowd on the top half of the poster, with the headline "Do you stand up for your rights . . ." The bottom half of the same poster showed former NFL player Colin Kaepernick kneeling with the headline ". . . or take a knee?"

Null reported that this poster "was vandalized and torn down" although it was replaced by the university. "The second poster, created by student Alyssa Gonzales, received the most feedback out of all of the posters." The rather primitive-style image showed Donald J. Trump holding a golf club walking in the opposite direction of a young boy lying dead by the beach, with his head in the water. A hat with the Puerto Rican flag on it sits beside him, and in the background, there is a tiny island with the Puerto Rican Flag. One professor stated that "he is not speaking against inclusion or for censorship, but the project of Trump was too graphic with the boy laying dead in the sand." It was based on the famous recent photograph of a young Syrian refugee boy lying washed up dead on a beach. Despite disagreements, ESU defended that this was a student project, and not about ESU taking a political stance on either side. At the forum some students expressed joy that the campus put their logo on the artwork to show that the students are being heard.

All the posters were displayed without captions or descriptions. "Heter said that this was to allow for people to get their own interpretation from it," Null wrote. "Then, about three to four days later, captions were put up beside the posters, along with the artist's intention."

The Inclusion Poster Project, according to ESU's provost Jo Bruno, was inspired by graphic designer Mirko Ilić's current Tolerance poster exhibition in circulation around the world. The purpose of this project was "to give students a platform to express their own views on inclusion," noted Heter, who added that the artists selected their own campus space to hang up their projects.

Responses coming from students, staff, and faculty were mixed, including tweets arguing that the university should not take a stance on political or controversial topics. "Many said that the university's logo should not have been placed in the corner of every poster," stated Null. The college president responded that "Logo only means it is an #ESU student project. . . . Not an #ESU position." The University replied with an email sent out Friday, stating, "While the posters are marked with the ESU logo, they are not a representation of the University's position, but rather our commitment to students' freedom of expression in the context of an intellectual and educational dialogue."

A student added that it was an uncomfortable image: "We're in college, and this is the place where we are supposed to feel uncomfortable." Null reported that after some students explained that the image of Trump "made them uncomfortable," the artist of the Trump painting revealed herself and spoke out saying, "life's uncomfortable." One of the artists taking part in the project insisted the work was "meant to invoke conversation."

"Only time will tell what will become of this ongoing development and the further outcomes of this ESU Inclusion Poster Project," concluded Null.

To view these posters, visit http://quantum.esu.edu/insider/poster-project-spreads-message-of-inclusion/.

# EXCLUSION
# BY DESIGN

- - - - - - - - - - - - - - - - - - - - - - - - - - - - -

**W**hat do Supreme Court Justice Oliver Wendell Holmes, Planned Parenthood founder Margaret Sanger, cereal inventor and wellness impresario Dr. John Harvey Kellogg, and American president Woodrow Wilson have in common? They are among the large number of Americans who, long before the Nazis adopted a euthanasia program to rid Germany of mental defectives, feeble-minded people, incurably ill people, and recidivist criminals, supported and propagated the "science" of eugenics. If you don't know what eugenics is by now, that is disappointing but not surprising. This widespread pseudoscientific movement sought to prove white supremacy over other skin pigment- and blood-based human "races" that they claimed were intellectually inferior.

Many respected Americans accepted eugenics. Justice Holmes wrote an 8–1 court decision that made forced sterilization federal law. Sanger advocated a program of breeding for "the gradual suppression, elimination and eventual extinction, of defective stocks." Kellogg believed that eugenic methods would help save the white race and supported racial segregation. As governor of New Jersey, Wilson signed a bill that forcibly removed reproductive rights from criminals or adults considered to be "feeble-minded" (in recent years his deep-seated racism has also come to light).

If you ever wondered why Native peoples were forcibly displaced from their lands; Jim Crow segregation went unchallenged in the South for so long; and miscegenation statutes were enacted in many states to prevent the legal marriage of and procreation by mixed-race couples, eugenics is the answer. As a movement it took hold in the United States in the late nineteenth and early twentieth centuries and was quickly exported to nativist, nationalist, and exclusionist nations that claimed their blood was pure blood.

"Eugenics" derives from Greek to mean "good birth." It is the application of genetic and heredity "science" as the basis for improving the human race and relegating those who do not fit the genetic schematic to second class (or lower) strata. The term eugenics was first coined by Francis Galton in the late 1800s. Originally, he determined that traits such as superior intelligence were hereditary and advocated selective breeding programs (a form of genetic engineering). This idea of building a master race was adapted as the Nazi Lebensborn breeding program.

American eugenics was championed by Charles Davenport, a respected biologist, and Harry Laughlin, a former teacher. In 1910, Davenport founded the Eugenics Record Office (ERO) at Cold Spring Harbor Laboratory in New York "to improve the natural, physical, mental, and temperamental qualities of the human family." The ERO assembled data about family traits, particularly interested in the inheritance of "undesirable aspects, such as mental disability, dwarfism, promiscuity and criminality." The list went on. The ERO remained active for three decades.

The first time I ever heard even a whisper about this hushed piece of American history was in a scene in Stanley Kramer's 1961 film *Judgment at Nuremberg* in which the actor Maximilian Schell as Hans Rolfe, defense lawyer for the four German judges on trial for their complicity and direct crimes during the Nazi era, including forced sterilization, quotes Justice Holmes who stated in one of the most infamous Supreme Court decisions, *Buck vs. Bell* (1927):

> It is better for all the world, if instead of waiting to execute degenerate offspring for crime, or to let them starve for their imbecility, society can prevent those who are manifestly unfit from continuing their kind. The principle that sustains compulsory vaccination is broad enough to cover cutting the Fallopian tubes. Three generations of imbeciles are enough.

This concept was directly attributable to the eugenicist thinking that prevaricated biological proof that a superior populace should procreate and to lay claim to a state of racial purity. Eugenics was also used to justify the lower-caste status and subjugation of native, minority, and racial "inferiors." The consequence of eugenics (which like some viruses is dormant but never really cured) is the fatally false notion of racial superiority that infected (and arguably still influences) everyday life, such as the authorship, illustration, and design of such seemingly innocuous 1941 books for children as *Our America: Little Stories for Young Patriots*. This volume attempts to teach the concept of inclusion and equality but is illustrated with the unexplained exclusion of non-white people. Eugenics was employed to ensure that white remained dominant (yes, even today).

# TYRANNY ILLUSTRATED

**F**rom inception, the United States has nurtured a motley share of homegrown autocrats and demagogues. Tyranny is an equal opportunity aspiration. American democracy arose from revolution against a despotic monarch yet never entirely expunged the tyrannical impulses hardwired in the original body politic. "We might be tempted to think that our democratic heritage automatically protects us from such threats," writes Timothy Snyder in *On Tyranny: Twenty Lessons from the Twentieth Century*. "This is a misguided reflex. In fact, the precedent set by the Founders demands that we examine the deep sources of tyranny, and to consider proper responses to it."

Shortly after Donald J. Trump was elected the forty-fifth president of the United States in 2016, Snyder, a professor of history and political scholar, wrote a pocket guide (what he calls a "pamphlet") for citizens of twenty telltale cautionary signs of tyranny and how to shield against them. At the 2017 annual staff meeting for the School of Visual Arts, the college's president David Rhodes pulled *On Tyranny* from his jacket breast pocket, recommending that everyone makes it an essential read. I did so that very day.

Although Snyder says that history may not repeat itself, it provides warning signs worth heeding. As a student of despotism of the early twentieth century, I vouch for the categorizations and examples he uses. Despots may espouse varied ideologies, including those focused on in his book, fascists, Nazis and communists, but tyrannies and tyrants share the same familiar methods, including narcissism, legal abuse, false patriotism, and fake news, to brainwash people and enforce and bolster their rule. All this and more is available in the hardcover book (or pamphlet) edition but brought home with even more fervency in the new version with illustrations by Nora Krug. Krug, the award-winning German-born author/illustrator of *Heimat* (Belonging). Published in 2020, *Heimat* is her quest to discover how her family lived in and somehow coexisted in Nazi Germany from 1933 through 1945.

"I cold-called her," Snyder explained in a phone interview. Although "I love everything about the original book" he believes the larger format and imagery of the graphic edition forces the mind to work differently. "You need art to imagine different futures. Pictures imagine different futures." By 2020 unthinkable futures for the United States were coming into focus, and although Snyder's polemical polemic is certainly persuasive enough, Krug's expressive interpretation gives *On Tyranny* even additional immediacy particularly for members of Gen Z, who will be soldiers (and hopefully defenders) in the next war on democracy.

# WHAT'S BLACK AND WHITE AND RE(A)D ALL OVER?

- - - - - - - - - - - - - - - - -

**T**he *New York Times*, where I proudly worked for over thirty years, has been the bulwark of freedom of free speech and expression in this nation. Blitzed by President Donald "fake news" Trump's bombast, the newspaper of record is holding its own in the battle for the First Amendment. Yet as Gay Talese wrote in his epic 1969 history of the paper, *The Kingdom and the Power*, "The years 1955 and 1956 were hardly ideal times for young reporters to be getting a start in the newsroom." The top management of the paper were distracted and disturbed at that time by the "intrusive tactics" of a McCarthy-era-inspired Senate subcommittee that was investigating purported communism in the press "and seemed determined to concentrate on the former Communists who were on the payroll of *The New York Times*."

The *Times* had sidestepped government and political scrutiny before, but "the dynamics of McCarthyism were still pervasive in the land." Among its news, composing, and pressroom staff there had been casual and active members of the Communist Party, which was usual in many media businesses (and their unions) during the 1930s and 1940s when the Soviet "Reds" were America's anti-Axis allies (CBS was particularly vulnerable but stood up to withering pressure). In the late 1930s Communist Party members working at the *Times* published a union-printed newspaper, *Real Times*, which aggressively criticized the paper's management for various perceived sins and supported white- and blue-collar union activism.

It was an awkward and embarrassing time for the paper, Talese reported, "one of suspicion and conflict, anger and compassion." The *Times* was divided into conservative super-patriots who resented colleagues who had been "exposed as one-time party members." There were staffers who "privately abhorred McCarthyism" but were more "cautious and remote in the newsroom" around those who were named before the investigating committee.

The head of the investigation, Mississippi senator James O. Eastland and his colleagues singled out the paper because the *Times* criticized segregation, challenged Congressional abuse of power, condemned McCarthyism, and rightly stood for the constitutional right of an accused individual to face an accuser. But publisher Arthur Sulzberger, according to Talese, called himself a "prejudiced witness for the capitalist system," and refused to retain a single Communist on the staff. He insisted that all employees subpoenaed before the committee must attend. Those *Times* men and women who were short-lived members and admitted their mistake were absolved, while those who took the Fifth Amendment were summarily fired.

In my early days at the *Times* in the early 1970s I knew staffers on both sides. I worked on the op-ed/editorial page with chief editor John Oakes, who, I was told and later read in Talese's book, was against the *Times'* rigid position on the Fifth Amendment and very much an advocate of "civil liberties and Bill of Rights." It is ironic that when I was hired for the op-ed page, I was warned that Mr. Oakes was rather conservative regarding the illustration proposed for the page. I had to show him the art almost every day, and indeed we did have a few disagreements over content and direction. But when I learned how he stood up against both Joe McCarthy and the Eastland Committee tactics, my high respect for him tempered the rebellious twenty-four-year-old tone I took when arguing about a drawing. Needless to say, I lost a few battles, but won some too. Mr. Oakes was a gentleman.

When I see the *Times* today stand up against the purposeful ravings of President Trump, thinking of those difficult days past when the nation and the paper were threatened by suppressive forces, I am both saddened and proud. Talese ends his chapter on this period in *The Kingdom and the Power* with an editorial statement that showed the *Times'* wisdom as authored by editorial board member Charles Merz:

> We cannot speak unequivocally for the long future. But we can have faith. And our faith is strong that long after Senator Eastland and his present subcommittee are forgotten, long after segregation has lost its final battle in the South, long after all that was known as McCarthyism is a dim, unwelcome memory, long after the last Congressional committee has learned it cannot tamper successfully with a free press, *The New York Times* will still be speaking for the men who make it, and only for the men who make it, and speaking, without fear or favor, the truth as it sees it.

# PART 3:
# PEOPLE

# ARCHIVES BY DESIGN

T he word *archive* evokes one idea with a variety of meanings.

An archive is a cataloged collection of past and present accomplishments that is structured in different ways for numerous purposes, including scholarship, reference, and preservation. Archives can be public, private, personal, institutional, professional, and cultural. They are wellsprings of history—the past and present as resources for the future. Archives are not only warehouses but also greenhouses for the nurturing of narratives. Out of archival seeds mighty stories grow.

There are many archives that exist or are currently in the making. However, there is limited space to house and experts to maintain them. Regardless of who or what comprises a specific archive, they cannot contain everything an individual or business has ever produced. The resources do not exist. So who decides what or who deserves preservation? It takes commitment and vision to divine what will make the cut, and sometimes wrong decisions are made. How often has valuable material been mistaken for inconsequential junk? What is extraneous is often essential and vice versa.

A proper archivist is a prospector who pans for archival gold, then filters it for essential raw material that scholars can interpret, shape, and transform into stories. Archivists rigorously search not only for perfect outcomes but also for the plans, notes, and iterations behind the outcome. In every bag or box, envelope or file, there's no greater satisfaction than when an archivist finds "gold in them thar hills." Invariably, the gold is valuable to everyone who has access to the archive.

One person's posterity is another's garbage. Printing and type samples, even when saved by their producers or creators as records of work, are not always preserved for long-term posterity. There comes a time where the output of an individual's, studio's, or business's work exceeds the ability to contain and catalog the artifacts that they've produced. The question of what to keep, what to dump and, more important, what to archive is a day of reckoning.

This symposium "Archives by Design" is conceived to address the increasing compulsions to 1. Preserve the histories of graphic design and illustration in all its varied manifestations and 2. Determine who, how, and why certain artifacts are deserving of preservation in an archival environment.

Not surprisingly, as design and illustration have become more integral to the writing, teaching, and understanding of history in general and have developed their own history, archives are increasing. Some are independently operated and others are folded into educational facilities. Archives are also burgeoning with the passing and aging of generations who are ready to release their work for scholarly and public use. In fact, the large number of practitioners finding permanently accessible homes for a growing number of legacies is far exceeding the ability to accept them, as the following chapter illustrates.

# UNLOVED?
# ART AS
# GARBAGE?

L ast week I received an email that has haunted me for reasons that will become clear. The missive explained that a passerby stumbled upon a pile of trash on 100th Street and Central Park West in New York City, including garbage bags containing numerous large ring binder portfolio books filled with original cartoons and illustrations. The passerby grabbed as many as possible and lugged them home to share with his wife. By coincidence, she happens to be friends with an artist pal of mine, to whom she sent an email in hopes of learning something about the creator of the discarded artwork. Included in the email were photos of the artwork, each signed with a name. My friend had no idea who the creator was, so she forwarded the photos to a friend of hers, a cartoonist, who is also a friend of mine. He did not recognize the artist either. So he decides to send the correspondence to me on the off chance I might know the artist, "because," he wrote in his email, "you know everyone." This is a flattering exaggeration, but . . . it turns out *I do* indeed know the artist, whose name is Bill Lee.

Not only did I know Bill Lee, but for many years we had a close working relationship and deep friendship. Bill was one of a new breed of satiric gag cartoonists. He had a singularly fluid linear style. He was also the humor editor of *Penthouse* and *Viva* magazines and he created one of my favorite comic sculptures: President Richard Nixon as a shrunken head, which he made into a poster that hung on my office wall. Bill also suggested the title of my second book, *Man Bites Man: Two Decades of Satiric Art*, in which his work was featured prominently.

I haven't seen Bill in over thirty years (such is the nature of living in New York), and I don't recall why we ended our friendship (such is the nature of memory loss). Nonetheless, I am convinced this sequence of totally random connections that triggered memories of Bill after three decades was somehow destined to be (such is the nature of paranormal energy).

That night I was trying *not* to think about the implications of this surprising sequence of events. The next day I contacted Ammon Shea, the man who salvaged and shared Bill's work with his wife, Alexandra Horowitz, who had written the email to Maira Kalman, who passed it on to Rick Meyerowitz, who forwarded it to me.

Ammon told me in an email that he removed only a very small selection of what was tossed. "My son and I were walking east on 100th between Columbus and Amsterdam last week, and noticed a man headed west, holding an armful of framed pictures," he recalled. "A hundred feet further on we came to a private sanitation truck, loading what looked to be the contents of someone's apartment into the back of the truck. It seemed obvious that someone had just passed away, and that their possessions were all being thrown away, without any concern."

"I saw a large portfolio," he added, "opened it and saw that it was filled with someone's art, and thought it was the sort of thing someone somewhere would be glad to see rescued. There were a couple of young men there going through the furniture, and I heard one say 'no, leave those behind . . . those are Polaroids . . . you need special equipment to look at them.' The 'Polaroids' turned out to be a set of binders, filled with Kodachrome slides. These were a mixture of travel pictures and slides of art, and so I grabbed these as well."

I suppose we have all seen art discarded in urban trash bins or town dumps. A librarian friend of mine, who has since passed away, made regular rounds of artist studios and the offices of creative institutions to collect discarded artifacts for his research library; he had collected some rare, important items. Over the years, I've salvaged pieces of value to me. I always wondered who and why someone would discard personal or professional creations in such an unceremonious manner. How did the art lose its value? Were they failed experiments? Was it an uncontrollable emotion—a release of frustration or anger? Or was the reason more prosaic—an existential shift in circumstance, like moving to smaller quarters or dying?

Whatever the reason, there is something sorrowful about the disposal of art, whatever the perceived quality. Among the material saved by Ammon and Alexandra were drawings from a trip Bill made to Poland to cover the Solidarity era in cartoons, possibly for *Penthouse*. There was a proposal for a charming book of fantasy, comic animal furniture that was inspired (Bill scribbled on one of them) by his young daughter. Who knows what other items were hauled away to heaven knows where?

Ammon concluded, "It is, I suppose, entirely possible that the decision to throw all this out was a considered one—I didn't know Bill Lee, and know nothing of the circumstances surrounding his works and their appearance on 100th Street. But I couldn't imagine just walking past the destruction of something that was once terribly important to someone without seeing if it could be otherwise handled."

I began seeking out clues to my estranged friend's whereabouts. I was impatient to find a rationale. I recalled that he had lived near 100th Street and CPW, where the bags were found. Before the pandemic I heard he was not in the best of health and required a caregiver to help him get around. I was given his telephone number, which I lost, though I found it on one of the discarded drawings. I dialed the exchange and an expressionless computer-generated voice immediately answered: "This number is no longer in service." Click.

I found no record of Bill's death on Google or Wikipedia. I found no personal website. Although he was often published, very few of his cartoons are archived online, even under the tag "Penthouse." I found a brief biography on a cartoonists' fan site and wrote to the site administrator but he could not help. "I never actually spoke to him," he admitted.

Next, I dug deep into my hazy memory for his daughter's name. It eventually came into focus, so I thought. I also thought she was a professor or college instructor outside of New York, and after a few frustrating hours clicking around faculty databases and trying out variations of the name, I stumbled on a possible match. In fact, I was so certain of it when I saw a photograph of a woman who resembled Bill that I wrote an email to her and waited. Two or three days went by without a word. I eventually looked in my spam folder and found that she had instantly responded:

*Hiya Steve,*

*This is indeed an odd story! I'm sorry to say, though, that I'm not [the person] you're looking for (there are SO MANY of us).*

I wrote to Maira to relate my brief search. She wrote back:

*Hi Dear Steve,*
*I'm sorry this has stirred up so many memories. Isn't that how it always is. You wake up in the morning and don't know what's going to hit you.*

Yes, it stirred up something. But more than faded memories, I am distressed that so much original artwork was relegated to the garbage heap. It is not possible to protect and save the gargantuan amounts of artifacts and documents that define an individual's life on earth; there is not enough time or space to store and care for it all. By this measure a creative life, unless rescued by chance or diligence, is easily reduced to just so much burdensome refuse.

Other than the mystery of not knowing whether Bill is alive or dead, I am haunted by the sad fact that he is just one of too many artists who were not archived or collected, and are now relegated to attics or, worse, a landfill. I am continually asked by many illustrators, cartoonists, and designers now in their seventies to nineties or their heirs who are responsible for the work where to deposit it and how to preserve it. I shrug. There are some museums, archives, libraries, and study centers that take donated materials; more extensive and historically significant collections are bought. But not everything can (or should) be saved. Not everything made by an artist has a measurable value. Still, this story provokes a sense of despair.

Preservation is validation. Validation is proof of life. Long ago, I published a fair amount of Bill's art. Other than what is in *Man Bites Man*, I do not have anything of his—and what I do have (somewhere) are photostats, anyway. Stored but not easily accessible. I am certain I saved a tattered copy of the Nixon shrunken-head poster. Maybe what remains of his work eventually will find an appreciative home—and maybe the best of it already has. Well, at least for now, some of it is off the street.

# FOREVER ART YOUNG

---

I dedicated my 1981 book *Man Bites Man: Two Decades of Satiric Art* to "Three Masters of the Comic Arts: Art Young, Gluyas Williams and Otto Soglow." If today I were instructed to only make one dedication (to save on typesetting costs, perhaps?), I would definitely choose Art Young—and not as you cynics might think, because this book is about Art Young, but because he is genuinely still a huge inspiration to me and lefties like me, and pillar of political cartoon history. For good measure I wouldn't even typeset his name. I'd simply show the cartoon that I ran in *Man Bites Man,* "From Jungle to Civilization," showing a pair of related beasts—an apprehensive old simian grasping an armful of coconuts and an anxious rich man tightly embracing bags of money. Although apes have not evolved much since his cartoon was drawn in the early twentieth century, today's ultra-wealthy have devolved into apes wearing polo shirts, designer jeans, and Tag Heuer watches rather than morning coats, cravats, and diamond tie pins. Otherwise, Young's cartoon is still on the money!

In fact, Art Young's brilliance as a cartoonist, satirist, and commentator is that he was always on the money; specifically on the well-heeled heels of those profit-mongering robber barons who amassed billions in wealth on the backs of labor. His most famous depiction of corporate excess and greed, titled "Capitalism" (published in *Life* 1911, then a humor magazine), portrays an obese, bald oligarch, gluttonously glugging from a drum-sized terrine, leaning back on a chair poised to topple off a cliff to the bottomless pit below. If one were to alter some physical characteristics to make him more contemporary looking, you've got the perfect visual indictment of today's Wall Street and Washingtonian plutocrat.

A lifelong provocateur, Young was of his time, ahead of his time, and timeless in terms of conceptual acuity and pictorial savvy. Nothing proves this better than *Art Young's Inferno.* Originally published in 1934, Young was influenced by Gustave Dore's exquisite 1861 engravings for *Dante's Inferno.* There have been several artist interpretations of the *Divine Comedy* in recent years, Gary Panter's *Jimbo's Inferno* (2006) and Seymour Chwast's adaptation (2010) among my favorites. However, nothing has come close to Young's roast of free-market capitalism and the venal capitalists, monopolists, and lobbyists who keep the fires stoked. In the role of Virgil, Young treats the viewer to hell as it had never been imagined but nonetheless exist(ed) to a large degree behind the facades of the towering office buildings and boardrooms then and now.

This was Young's final visit into Satan's den before he died in 1943 (and I'm almost certain arose to cartoonist heaven). He made two iterations before this.

His first in 1892, *Hell Up To Date: The Reckless Journey of R. Palasco Drant, Newspaper Correspondent, Through the Infernal Regions, As Reported by Himself,* does not so much hit the hotspots of capitalism as it uncovers the secrets of the mythical underworld and what it takes to become a resident. The second, the 1901 *Through Hell With Hiprah Hunt,* was a reprise rendered in a less fussy, more mature line. Drant was replaced by the Bible-thumping preacher Hunt—Presbyterian through and through. The savagely funny imagery is a direct precursor of the Sixties underground comix.

Of course, Young was not alone in his disdain for capitalism. He was art editor for *The Masses,* whose offices were just a handful of blocks from where I am writing this (and nearby locales where some of those early underground papers and comics were published), and oversaw the work of other strong, strident, and witty cartoonists and illustrators, including Robert Minor, Boardman Robinson, William Gropper, Rockwell Kent, and others with razor-sharp pens. He was preceded by artists for the French *L'Assiette au Beurre* and German *Simplicissimus* who lampooned their very own fat cats without mercy.

Speaking of mercy. It is merciful that Art Young, despite a few brushes with the censors, was able to create his Inferno master work. So many decades after publication, the dire threats to America's well-being that Young predicted in the corruption of health care, real estate, industrial monopolies, public services, and, of course, politics and government are all too real. I wonder were he to return to our times would Young be shocked or bemused. Would he and Bernie Sanders be comrades? Would he embrace the Green New Deal (*Art Young's Inferno* was published on the eve of FDR's New Deal)? Or would he simply say "I showed you so"? After all, his cartoon charting the economic status of the nation, "Poor" / "Out of Poverty"/ "Rich"/ "Richer" is beyond prescient. Truth, I suppose, is often not funny.

# BARRY BLITT'S FERVENT IMAGERY

**B**arry Blitt's intelligent absurdity, fervent skepticism and memorable comic imagery are graphically charged detonations against the power brokers, politicians, influence peddlers, and raging horde of illiberal aggressors who frighten, repress, and besiege us with their false patriotism and greedy corruption. Deploying his disarmingly modest graphic style, his famous (and infamous) *New Yorker* covers have brilliantly attacked over two decades of folly and hypocrisy. But that is only one part of his collected body of work. He has also produced scores of little-known and less iconic, though no less acerbic, illustrations and cartoons for scores of publications not principally known for their political content.

Despite appearances, Blitt is not a subversive. Rather he is an all-around image-maker: an illustrator, cartoonist and caricaturist—and author of his own ideas. He wields his wit for both critique and commentary, but always to trigger a visceral reaction. Wherever his drawings appear, his humor offers a kind of liberation, if only for a moment, from the oppressive news cycles and their perpetual touting of political idiots and ideological idiocy. Blitt's comically incendiary drawings have been so effective at precisely piercing the thin skin of the powerful that he has garnered accolades and scorn often from the same target. There can be no disputing that Blitt has earned a vaunted place in the pantheon of twenty-first-century political satire alongside Edward Sorel, Ralph Steadman, Robert Osborn, Jules Feiffer, and Robert Grossman, through output that covertly or overtly defames the unscrupulous and defangs the infamous.

"I would hope my work is more observational," he once told me. "What could be more boring than partisan satire? I really don't think it makes a difference what my politics are—I'm probably to the left of center on most issues—but in my work I'm looking for ridiculousness and hypocrisy wherever I can find it." To describe him only as a political artist and provocateur is much too limiting. In an era drowning in digital noise and visual static, it may be more accurate to say that Blitt's virtue is cutting through the incomprehensible, conceiving pictures that engage his audience with whatever theme he tackles and wherever they are ultimately published.

Looking back through his early work, it appears Blitt was not born with a taste for satiric blood. It developed as he realized that his drawings mattered to others. I've known him for over two decades, long enough to recall when his fledgling work was much more on the light, sketchy side and his conceptual self-confidence was more tentative than it is today. In answer to a statement I had written that he was one of the most strident illustrators of the early 2000s, he responded with typical cheekiness: "As a small child I drew pictures in my room dreaming of becoming one of the more comically strident illustrators of the 2000s." He added more seriously, however, that in truth "I am still very tentative, work-wise and everything-wise." While getting published in major magazines throughout the country had to have emboldened him, nonetheless "I still have to force myself with every drawing and every sketch to not hold back, to not be too timid on the page."

In his mature work Blitt does not "hold back," but neither does he overplay his cards, picture-wise. Some illustrator-satirists pour their conceptual guts on the paper. What distinguishes Blitt from some of his peers is his loose pen line, outlining or containing subtle watercolor hues. As biting as it may be, the visual appearance of his work is more sublime and soothing—unthreatening might be apt—than rabid and raucous. When looking at some of his interpretive observations, like the aviary in the chapter titled "Heading South," I see a curiously original coupling of the fantastical Edward Lear and the trenchant George Grosz—the lyricism of one and the expressionism of the other. It is this well-balanced combination of elegance and power that defines his distinct brand of nuanced irony.

Once, in a conversation we had, Blitt implied that much of his best work was the result of accidents that somehow succeeded. I don't believe that for a minute. A visual satirist is incapable of hitting as many bulls-eyes as he has done throughout this volume without being disciplined. While accidents obviously happen, discipline is knowing when and how to capitalize on them—it takes mastery to use opportunity. What looks ad hoc cannot really be ad hoc. Arguably, line for line, brushstroke for brushstroke, for years Blitt has hit his moving targets as much or more than comparable name-brand artists—and his hit-rate does not rely entirely on the comic drawing virtues of his pictures alone.

Blitt's effectiveness as a topical commentator is his virtuosity with words and pictures. Often words are redundant, other times they are an additional jolt to the joke or concept. Both components are consistently in sync in his work, regardless of how simple the words. Take "All I Want For Christmas: Young Elites and Their Holiday Wishes," created during the Bush era. What could be funnier or, for that matter, more disarming than reading "Billy O'Reilly's or L'il Hillary Clinton's" wishes while seeing the beguiling images together? Blitt's wit comes through simply in the title of "Rejected New Nicknames for Sean 'Puff Daddy' Combs"—how can that be ignored? And when it comes to absurd-reality, the off-the-wall comedy of "Cellular Phones of the Future" notably the "Talk 'n' Shoot" cellphone and pistol combo is spot-on hilarity. His word and picture conceptual combos are one-two punches to the head.

During World War II, Germany ravaged its foes through blitzkrieg, lightning bombardments on defenseless cities. Although it is not as lethal, what might be referred to as Blittskrieg is Blitt's keen ability to make satire to attack an issue that both devastates the target and leaves the rest of us smiling. Viva Blitt, may Blittskrieg continue.

# THE JAWS
# OF SATIRE

C aricature is Steve Brodner's weapon of choice. Aimed with precision accuracy, his satiric barbs pierce the facades of strongmen and their stooges who deceive and delude. His work draws its strength, in part, from a keen ability to harness wit and humor. While lesser illustrator-cartoonists use clichés as substitutes for original ideas, Brodner uses common references from past and present popular culture to challenge folly and eviscerate the powerful. Take, or instance, the famous film poster for Jaws, showing the giant man-eating shark soaring upward like an undersea missile, just inches away from an unsuspecting, soon-to-be-consumed bather. Like other symbols in Brodner's repertoire of cultural mnemonics, this is a startling reminder of danger, evil, and fear.

Brodner's appropriation of the Jaws image was the cover of the *Village Voice* at the moment when candidate Donald J. Trump began to attack and consume his GOP rivals. Following the metaphor to a logical conclusion, it suggested that Trump, who began as a small fish in a big pond, had grown into a serious threat to all the Republicans drowning in the choppy primary sea.

"The idea behind [this] caricature," Brodner explained at the time, "is to use Trump's fearsome features in relation to the killer shark to bring out what is perhaps unseen under the surface of a face." Exaggeration is only one tool for telegraphing a strong message to the largest number of people. When Brodner is on the hunt, his goal is to reach a large audience far and wide. His metaphoric visual language allows him to capture attention while inflicting satiric damage.

Steve Brodner (b.1954) began political cartooning in 1976 for the *Hudson Dispatch* in Hudson County, New Jersey. Although not the most satisfying job, it provided him with an insatiable appetite for graphic political commentary. Between 1979 and 1982 he self-published the *New York Illustrated News*. All the while honing his skills and sharpening his blade, he worked for *Harper's*, *The Progressive*, the *New York Times*, and later *Esquire*, the *New Yorker*, and most major periodicals (and on video podcasts too). Brodner realized the power of his pen and that in the right circumstances, the cartoon can make opinion-altering differences, or at least affirm existing beliefs. His primary model in his early years was the pioneering mid to late 1800s Bavarian-born American cartoonist and caricaturist Thomas Nast, whose linear cross-hatched style Brodner faithfully copied at the time.

After being so strongly influenced by Thomas Nast, Brodner transitioned out of the stylistic shadows into a decidedly original "Brodner approach," shifting from stiff line to fluid watercolor almost overnight. When and what, I recently asked him, was the aha moment that triggered the pivot? "The moment I remember was a specific assignment for the *National Lampoon* to illustrate an 'Alice in Wonderland' parody called 'Alice in Regularland' by P. J. O'Rourke," Brodner recalled. "Prior to that I had been so moved by the work of nineteenth-century cartoonists, Nast in particular, that I absolutely believed that work of that kind, given that level of extreme care and attention would be similarly powerful in our time." However, as Brodner was "doing this goof" on the (original Victorian) John Tenniel's work he came to the realization that this approach was much too derivative. "What I had seen as dynamic and biting, [readers] saw as a quaint, antique curio, the very last thing I wanted."

Also magazines were using color much more, and Brodner was forced to figure out how to get there, never having painted anything before. Gradually, he made his way into watercolor, teaching himself by way of colored pencil. "Drawing with color was, for me, a gateway into watercolor. I kept on using pen and ink for black and white assignments but experimented with different line approaches, but always respecting the line much more. And, yeah, realizing at last that we were in the century of Grosz and Picasso and Ronald Searle," he adds.

Throughout history caricature has been the bedrock of political and social satire. Brodner is today one of a handful of illustrators who continued this legacy. I wondered how he perceives his contribution now and in the future? "Satire will carry on," he says. "Right now it is bigger than ever. Not always for the best though. Where it used to be that to do satire you needed a publisher and an editor (who might vet the work) now the Internet is a free-for-all. There isn't the space to allow for pauses and quiet moments that could create a moment for a quiet joke or a bit of irony that can grow into a laugh. No time for reflection. We now do one-liners and they'd better be fast and not about obscure references." Yet despite the negatives, Brodner does not worry about his legacy. "I feel I have to do the best work I can do, tell the truth and go to bed. People tell me that it matters to them that I make pictures. I am very lucky if that is true. It's all that matters: telling the truth. We are swimming in bullshit. I can't think of a more important thing for anybody to do."

The old canard, however, is that art does not change people's minds but reinforces existing beliefs and provides a laugh or two. "I never feel that a piece of art is in the running to change anyone's mind," Brodner agrees.

Watch how culture works. Conditions change making absurd ideas, suddenly possible. Could FDR have won in '28? No. Could Reagan in '68? No. Could you walk into a party in 1957 and tell people that they shouldn't be smoking? No. Remember Clinton and gays-in-the-military debate? It destroyed his poll ratings in his first three months in office. Do you hear anybody now saying that we cannot have a gay president? Look now at the climate denial position. It is melting almost as fast as the Arctic. And then there's weed! Times change. So to me, the question is: how do they actually do that? I think reality catches up with culture finally. And the culture reflects reality in many ways. During the Vietnam War the anti-war movement was boosted by, not only rock music, but also underground comics, TV comedians, comedy records, political cartoons in newspapers, political art in magazines, graphic designers, movies, posters etc. So the graphic arts is a part of mass media that cannot, in my view, be singled out as separately responsible for the movement of culture. . . . But remember this, satire has no power at all if it isn't true. Drawing a swastika on Trump's forehead would be meaningless, until one understands how much power the racist right has derived from his various forms of support.

Caricature can be a useful weapon or an entertainment. And the role of caricature today as Brodner sees it is significant to the extent it is published and appears before peoples' eyes. "We have many truly great ones all making a difference. Their work forces you to consider an idea. Barry Blitt in the *New Yorker*, Victor Juhasz and Anita Kunz in *Rolling Stone*, Edel Rodrigues and Tim O'Brien in *Time*. And still about 50 editorial cartoonists, some employed on papers and some winging it on the net and in syndication." He pauses while going through his mental Rolodex and is reminded of important work coming from Canada, Europe, the Americas, the Middle East. "Many risking their lives to draw. We are not making the kind of money we used to but we are making art and it is being seen. And much of it will stand with the best of all time," he says.

Brodner has taught satiric art as part of a larger menu of approaches at SVA for some time. What, then, are the attitudes and commitments of current students toward satire and art in general as curative or aide-mémoire? "I have students who love children's books, fantasy stories, personal memoir, humorous articles, young adult fiction. And then there are the artists who come to me with the gene to do caricature and satire," he explains. "It is hard no matter what the topic is because of one basic reason, compression: how to jam all the necessary elements in the composition and make it super-clear and beautiful at the same time. To then put on top of that the task of representing a political point of view, without being obtuse, dilute, corny, crass, under- or-overcooked, wrong? I am amazed at what they do. I love my kids. But they must have the gene."

About his own genes, he speaks excitedly of his most famous work, which in its time was the poster for the Warren Beatty film *Bulworth* (1998). The film wasn't a hit, but the image got a great deal of play and Brodner was very closely associated with it. There were not many illustrated movie posters at that time, and his stood out and won a lot of awards. "I believe it was a very good film, by the way, and one that has grown in esteem over time. However, I still wonder, how could anyone expect to make blockbuster comedy about campaign finance, produced by Fox? (Beatty to me: 'I really don't care. I'm a rich guy.')" Another is "The Combover" for the *Nation* (2015), the drawing with the Nazi swastika etched onto Trump's head: "It nailed Trump's racism early on and then became a fixture on social media. It was printed out and used as a banner at rallies, projected on walls, etc. I believe the extreme nature of it is more justified every week." And then "The Trump Ring" (2019) for the *Washington Post* got a great deal of response on social media and was shared more than anything Brodner has ever done. Soon after it ran, the Mueller Report was whitewashed "for the propaganda purposes of the Trump/Fox media machine," he says. "This piece stands as a document, by itself, of the Russian attempt to sway an election and influence Donald Trump and his circle of goons."

This is a critical moment in Brodner's career. "I am in the weird position of having done everything I wanted to in this field," he says proudly. "I have been a regular contributor at top publications, given relatively free rein to say what I have wanted. Covers, full pages, spreads of my own ideas, traveling journalist [about fifty on-location stories] cartoons, comics, TV, film, blogs, social media, political art shows with colleagues, web series . . ." He pauses, then adds wistfully: "Here's the problem: I feel I am just starting. Every day I wish I could have another crack at getting it down better. Hey, let's try this! Every day new horrors emerge that need to be treated in pictures. Who can sleep?"

# THANKS, ROBERT GROSSMAN, FOR YOUR RABID WIT

**A** month or so before he passed away in his sleep on Thursday, March 15, 2018, I had dinner with Robert Grossman (1940–2018). True to his witty, acerbic, satiric self, he had those of us around the table in stitches as he recited his impromptu lyrics for a comic song about Donald J. Trump. He was genius at making anything rhyme and make comedic relevance too. I wish I had a recording device on the ready—or at least a better functional memory—because as usual his words were hilariously biting. Sadly, I don't remember a single phrase. Bob had spot-on verbatim recall of just about any passage from any text he'd ever read that he then related to almost any topic of current interest. He had an amazing memory and an incredible ear and eye for topical humor—that, along with a firm grasp of history would make your head spin with delight.

Bob's humor was of the infectious variety. His most recent comic strip, "TWUMP and POOTY," a send-up of Punch and Judy, however, was never picked up by any magazine, so I ran them on *The Daily Heller* (printmag.com/daily-heller/twump-pooty-story-date-robert-grossman/). It is hard to believe that when Bob's wit was needed most, it was ignored by today's press. Our loss!

Bob's death was unexpected. I felt kicked in the stomach when on Friday morning I read an email from his companion, Elaine Louie, announcing the tragic news. Certainly, there will be a slew of memorials, celebrations, and recollections about his life and art. He was not just good; he forever commands an essential place in caricature and satire history—and American humor, in general. So, for my part, this is not the obituary to lionize him, rather it is a thank-you, Bob.

Thank you for all the work that made our powerful figures look mockingly absurd when they deserved it and poignantly human when they didn't. Thank you for visual treats like your irreverent "Babe Lincoln." Thank you for all those conceptually resplendent transfigurations of Richard Nixon, Ronald Reagan and George Bush, not to mention your tweaks on Monica Lewinsky, Hillary Clinton, and dozens upon dozens more famous and infamous. Thanks for your enlightening conversations and dissertations on just about anything I can imagine. And thanks for never turning down a job I offered you, no matter how minor—it was major for me. Oh and thanks for the caricature-sculpture you did of me.

The Brooklyn-born Grossman's father was a sign painter. This may contribute to why, when Bob decided after graduating from Yale and working on its humor magazine to switch from gag cartoons to his more iconic illustrative method, with the common airbrush as his tool of choice. The airbrush was not new. Commercial artists had used it since the late nineteenth century—mostly for retouching but figuratively too—but Grossman transformed its smooth, streamlined gradients into a style, method, and unprecedented art form that altered the look of illustration in the 1960s. Others followed suit, but Grossman's allure was not just style. He applied the balloon-like airbrush aesthetic to the serious themes in politics, race, religion, corruption, etc. His Nixon with a fold-out Pinocchio nose (with Henry Kissinger as Jiminy Cricket on its end) for the cover of *National Lampoon* was one of the most savagely funny Watergate protests and possibly the most memorable. Bob knew better than anyone of his generation how to make ridicule that skewered its target while making the rest of his audience apoplectic with joy.

There are so many brilliant (and that word does not do them justice) caricatures (and sculptures) Bob made of the famous and infamous in all walks of life, that one has to see them to believe how prodigious and indefatigable he was and how completely committed he was to the art.

When anyone dies, the finality of that presence is palpable. But when someone dies who had and continued to have so much talent to give, it is devastating. Bob's passing will take time to reconcile, but his work is online and waiting to be made into a book. For many of us, certain pieces will continue to trigger memories of times and places, people, and events. Bob Grossman's art allows me to remember when illustration was profound and Bob was among the most profound of them all.

# MARSHALL ARISMAN, SHAMAN AND TRICKSTER

‗ ‗ ‗ ‗ ‗ ‗ ‗ ‗ ‗ ‗ ‗ ‗ ‗ ‗ ‗ ‗ ‗ ‗ ‗ ‗

**I**t is as hard to reconcile Marshall Arisman's drawn, painted, and sculpted imagery—its yin of intensity and yang of spirituality—with the serene man whom I've known for many decades. However, Marshall's mystique is his duality. In public he is calm and calming, an erudite raconteur, insightful teacher, and generous counselor. On canvas, paper, and clay he is the trickster, shaman, and mystic who sees auras and experiences the paranormal. Arisman devoted a lifetime to seeking a balance between mortality and immortality, a state of spiritual harmony that underlies and defines existence. He often said of his art that he liked to "amuse himself" by making images that derived from his subconscious; in fact, he was looking for answers to existential questions. I hope he found what he was looking for when he unexpectedly and suddenly passed into the unknown on a beautiful Friday afternoon.

When David Rhodes, President of School of Visual Arts, informed me about the heart that attacked my friend of fifty years, he said "nothing good happens on Fridays." That resonates for me. I see Fridays as an end; the end of a week is *not* the beginning of a weekend. Friday afternoon is a kind of nether place where tragic or wonderful things happen. You never can predict. It is always a stressfully anxious day—this one was filled with sadness.

Marshall's passing is incredibly painful for his wife Dee Ito—with whom he shared everything—and for those friends, students, and colleagues who were drawn into his orbit by design or happenstance. He leaves a void that while impossible to fill is, however, overflowing with memories that will last many lifetimes.

I've attempted to write a conventional, objective obituary about Marshall—pertinent place and dates, accomplishments, and anecdotes—but I cannot detach myself from our long and cherished relationship. To say he altered my existence is made even more vivid—and heartbreaking—by his absence. So, here are a few of the many unforgettable moments.

Marshall expelled me from SVA. He had to. I rarely attended class. I was enrolled to get a draft deferment. I was working anyway, and when he saw my portfolio of published work, as primitive as it was, he offered me a deal to graduate from SVA and retain my deferment. He called my job as cartoonist and so-called art director of an "underground" newspaper "work study." He said he would allow the job to earn me enough credits to advance to the senior year, "only if you attend classes," he emphasized.

Marshall was not what I expected of a department chairperson. I had already experienced the cold bureaucratic kind at NYU, and Marsh's kind and empathetic persona took me off guard. We chatted about illustration, art (the quality and lack thereof in my own work), and the Vietnam-era politics that was driving us all. I was so chill after our talk that he convinced me to accept his offer. I can only imagine how many others he treated in a similar way—how many lives he saved or encouraged. A few days after I emerged from his spell, I did, however, reject the plan. Instead, I commissioned him to do covers for one of the papers I worked for. A friendship ensued with Marsh, Dee, and me. I didn't see that coming but it seems so natural in retrospect. That's what Marshall was about. I know I was not alone.

A few years later, he asked if, given my experience with newsprint, I would like to teach a class that would result in the SVA student paper, *AIR* (Artist In Residence). I accepted, but it didn't last long. Marshall then approached me with his concept for developing a new graduate program entitled MFA Illustration: The Illustrator as Visual Journalist. I agreed to lecture on the history of illustration over two semesters. I had once wanted to be a historian; lack of schooling squelched that goal, but Marshall didn't seem concerned that I would learn on the job. He had faith. I was nourished by his faith. Marshall had a divine power, I thought then and still believe today. Our friendship grew exponentially after 1984 when the MFA began to function after two years of preparation. Fourteen years later, when Lita Talarico and I cofounded the MFA Design/ Designer as Author department (now entering its twenty-fifth year), I promised to stay on at MFA Illustration. I did for only one semester, but Marsh and I remained close friends.

Marshall was responsible for my third and final marriage (now in its 39th year) to Louise Fili. Unbeknownst to me, he arranged for us to both be jurors for an illustration competition at SVA. He knew exactly what he was doing when he suggested I walk her home. I was always skeptical of his mystical tendencies, but he somehow saw our auras were in sync. Marshall was either a good medicine man or simply cagey; it didn't matter.

Marshall was a trickster who questioned, subverted, and mocked authority and convention. Just a month ago, he admitted to a trick he had played on me decades earlier. Whether he was mysteriously anticipating his demise and thought he should reveal this before it was too late or he was just playfully, albeit cunningly, toying with my brain. He enjoyed doing that with everyone, I don't have a clue: He spoke in that unmistakably calm Arisman voice. He reminded me of a trip we made together to lecture at a conference at Marshall University in Huntington, West Virginia, in the late 1980s. "There were two ways of traveling; one was a direct flight in a regular jet, the other was a small puddle-jumper prop plane," he began. "They would arrive within an hour of each other. I had my travel agent make the reservations, who told me the options." He paused and with a guilty smile revealed "I knew how terrified you were about flying [and he was right] so I thought for a minute, weighed the possibilities, and told her to book the puddle-jumper. I never told you, I thought it best." I was indeed terrified.

That is the tip of Marshall Arisman—the yin and yang; the tricky and sensible; the inspiring and artful; the loyal and compassionate. He was sly and clever enough to add spice to the lives of everyone who loved him.

# CHRISTOPH NIEMANN'S CREATIVE POWER

I t takes special creative agility to produce editorial illustrations that transcend ephemerality yet capture the essence of a particular moment, to turn abstract marks into signs, glyphs, symbols, characters, and conceptions that compellingly impact the emotions and intellect of an audience, to channel the right image at the right time for the right result. Christoph Niemann is blessed with this gift. It is anyone's guess how his incredible fluency with the language of symbolic and metaphoric imagery was so expertly honed—and in such a relatively short time, too. Being a romantic, I like to believe that he (and a few others like him) was placed on Earth with creative powers that allow him to "speak" in universal visual tongues for the benefit of humankind. Nonetheless, I have no explanation for why these powers reside with him, so it remains a mystery worthy of investigation.

We know that Niemann is indeed the product of the reputable State Academy of Fine Arts in Stuttgart, Germany, and that one of his mentors there was the late, great Heinz Edelmann. Yet many other illustrators went through the same process without achieving the same "chosen" status. In the world of applied art there are *illustrators*, and then there are illustrators. The best of the former are adept at the difficult feat of visualizing ideas in iconic ways. The best of the latter go a few steps further by digging deep into the viewer's perceptions. As an interpreter of political, social, and cultural issues and events, Niemann uses pictures to untangle the inevitable jumble of confusions that confound the average brain. His drawings clarify the chaos, which enables readers to better comprehend various levels of complexity.

In the late 1990s, I was art director at the *New York Times Book Review*, and Paula Scher introduced me to her summer intern—Christoph Niemann. I immediately realized that this was no ordinary illustrator/designer. Although a trifle "gawkward," he was surprisingly articulate about art and its role as a mass communication tool. He had a mature understanding of the power of pictures and the difference between how gags and commentaries worked in driving public opinion and comprehension. (We were both Knicks fans, too, and that was just one aspect of the kinship he had with American culture.)

Yet these initial impressions, nice as they were, gave no indication to how special and, later, integral to my professional life he would become. Niemann had yet to actually perform his magic. But perform he soon did. Even minor assignments resulted in a barrage of great ideas (or "idears," as he called them). I came to almost slavishly rely on his capacity to come to my rescue whenever I was stuck. Most times, I did not have to utter a word of direction; when I did, it was usually superfluous. He would have a solution to the problem before I even finished telling him what it was. Over the phone, I could hear the dopamine in his brain pumping away. Within minutes, sketches poured out from the nearby fax machine, each one slightly more spot on than the last—and not just refinements of one idea but often a half-dozen distinct concepts.

Niemann was a veritable illustration Superman, able to leap beyond the clichés of regurgitated editorial subject matter with a single bound. Though disguised as an unassuming, tall, lanky, bespectacled nerd (sorry, Christoph), he had such sophisticated translation skills for a kid in his early twenties that I was awestruck by his almost flawless capacity to forgo the obvious and by force of will pull from his head original images, perfectly conceived. Over the few years we worked together, I watched as his conceptual capabilities exponentially increased every time another art director at another publication employed his gifts. "My destination is no longer a place, rather a new way of seeing," wrote Marcel Proust, as if to describe the essence of Niemann's speedy evolution.

"My work has changed quite a bit since I started, in format, style, and approach," Niemann says. "All these changes have felt personal and subjective. But when I look back, I see that they have followed larger trends in the industry: from the idea-driven editorial assignments of the late '90s to the early 2000s, to the 'illustrator as author' essays of the 2000s to the 2010s, to the idea of working directly with an audience next to the established platforms of magazines, newspapers, and books."

In this self-estimation, Niemann is characteristically modest. While I consider his rise to be meteoric, and his status among the all-time greats inarguable, he has always been much more restrained about his development and his talents. When I suggest that the reason he is so routinely on target is because he harbors a vast and innate reservoir of ideas, he says, "I don't have a store of ideas, sadly. What I do have is a store of images that I run through and that I try to combine in unexpected ways. The challenge is to update that store of images, because visually and culturally the world constantly changes."

Fair enough, but his thought process must be lightning fast, no? "This process of recombining these images and ideas is slow and unsexy," he says. "I go through endless nonsensical iterations before something like an idea forms itself. And to make sure an idea actually does make sense, I need to stare at it for quite some time. The proverbial aha moment is what the reader should experience when they end up looking at the piece—for me it has precious little relevance when creating.

"I'm not sure if I can really think that well visually," he says. "In order for an idea to come to life, it needs to grow on paper—or a screen. Sometimes, of course, a visual idea forms in my head, but these are usually just reiterations of things I've done or seen in the past. New things only start happening in the drawing process."

Regardless, there are so many trains of thought leaving his mental station that choosing or editing the best option for an illustration is probably his biggest challenge. He says that when it comes to editing, "Nothing beats putting a concept away for a day or two and looking at it with a fresh set of eyes." One way for him to select from his storage bank is "to rely on a small set of friends that I run things by. And I know that working with art directors over the years has benefited my work tremendously, even though at times they might fail to see the greatness of every single sketch I send them."

If Niemann refuses to be boastful, I will on his behalf: He is a conceptual drawing machine. "Since all the work I do involves drawing, I don't have to force myself to draw," he once told me. "But recently I've found that it is very important to take more time to draw aimlessly—as an exercise, but also just to see what happens." This perhaps accounts for the extensive range of approaches he uses; another explanation is that he doesn't want to be locked into one style. "I studied graphic design," he explains, "and that approach has informed the way I illustrate: A designer wouldn't start with a typeface. You start with the idea, and then choose the right assets to make the idea come to life. I try to do the same with images. I've come to appreciate the power of keeping my artistic vanity in check."

Speaking of vanity, he says what drives him—"maybe out of a youthful sense of insecurity"—is the audience's reaction. "Whether you get through to a reader with an editorial drawing about interest rates or a watercolor drawing of a tree doesn't make much of a difference to me."

In recent years, Niemann has been creating what I call "environmental" interventions—images that build on objects, photographs, and other real-life elements. These started as visual exercises, done out of his belief that so much of what an artist does is see images in a new way. "Eventually though, a certain routine sets in, and you develop a more predictable approach," he says. "When I think of a chair, the image that pops up in my head is some bland stock photo version of a chair. Through this exercise, I want to challenge that stock photo image in my mind and force myself to really see objects. How do the elements line up when you look at them from a slightly different angle? How does real-world lighting affect the shape and volume?"

Niemann is riding on the crest of a mighty wave. His illustrations appear everywhere, and he is developing his own expressive projects. "I want to further explore what happens when I apply this open-ended approach of visual experiments to slightly more involved projects," he says. "I've found that in order to be able to experiment, though, I need to be the one who operates the machinery. So the most important task is: I need to learn a lot more." He learns, and his audience learns along with him.

# CIPE PENELES, FIRST WOMAN OF DESIGN

I was a thirty-ish-year-old art director when Cipe (short for Ciporah) Pineles, an Austrian Jewish émigré, invited me to critique her magazine design class at the Parsons School of Design in New York. What an honor. For years before meeting her at her pied-à-terre on East 9th Street, I heard glowing things about her career. She was a legend, not just because she was married to the legendary Austrian-émigré designer Will Burtin and later CBS design director Bill Golden. Or because she assisted Turkish-born Condé Nast art director M. F. Agha. She earned her props not from associations with these other eminences in a male-dominated design field, but because she was herself an eminence—indeed a pioneer—in a profession that had yet to experience its overwhelming demographic shift. She did not become a pioneer by chance either. It wasn't easy even for the most hard-nosed woman to do.

Cipe Pinelas was the first woman admitted to the Art Directors Hall of Fame. By 1943 it was about time. Women were designers and art directors.

The announcement for "An Evening with One of the Best," a lecture series in the late 1980s sponsored by the Art Directors Club of New York, promised to be an illuminating conversation with six veteran advertising art directors and graphic designers. The title of the evening was not false advertising, but the event was more than a little tainted. The participants were all men. Once upon a time, few would have raised an eyebrow at this, but when these evenings were held in the late 1980s, women had already become the majority gender, if not in advertising, then in graphic design. One woman who should have definitely been invited to participate was Cipe Pineles (1910–1995). As art director of *Glamour*, *Overseas Woman*, *Seventeen*, and *Charm*, the Viennese-born Pineles had as much, if not more, influence on publication design and illustration in America as any member of the Art Directors Club.

In 1948 Pineles became the first female member of the New York Art Directors Club (founded in 1921) and was eventually the first woman inducted into the Art Directors Hall of Fame. That she broke the sex barrier was indeed the reason for receiving a two-column obituary (with a photograph) in the *New York Times*, an honor usually reserved for individuals who have made lasting lifetime achievements. Although Pineles would have vehemently denied that this was an accomplishment on which to hang a legacy, it certainly was significant at a time when men—young and old—jealously guarded the gates to the exclusive sanctum. Pineles was proposed for membership in the late 1930s but was repeatedly turned down until, the story goes, her first husband, William Golden (she was also married to Will Burtin) refused to join, saying that he wanted no part of a men's club. Pineles was admitted the next day.

As a Pratt graduate, Pineles started looking for work in the early 1930s, landing a job with Contempora, a consortium of internationally renowned designers, artists, and architects, where she designed modish fabric designs and displays. In 1933 she was hired as an assistant to Dr. M. F. Agha, art director of *Vanity Fair* and *Vogue*, where, as a novice at publication design, she received an invaluable education from this brilliant taskmaster. "We used to make many versions of the same feature. If we did, let's say, twenty pages on beauty with twenty different photographers we made scores of different layouts in order to extract every bit of drama or humor we could out of that material. Agha drove us to that because he was never happy with just one solution. And he was right too. We learned that magazine design should never play second fiddle to advertising," Pineles explained. Five years later she was appointed art director at *Glamour*, a poor relation to *Vogue*, targeted at women who couldn't afford the high cost of dress-up. Pineles was told that while money was no object at *Vogue*, at *Glamour* she'd have to do whatever she could on a meager budget. She made the proverbial silk purse, but was so indignant over Condé Nast's demeaning posture over this magazine that she left *Glamour* in 1944 to become art director of *Overseas Woman*, an army magazine for American servicewomen stationed abroad. From there she moved to *Seventeen*, a magazine that defined the teenage market for girls.

"That was the best job I had because the editor was attuned to the audience, and no matter what anybody else did, she and I knew that for seventeen-year-olds the subjects had to be done in a special way," Pineles recalled. She personalized her art direction in the sense that if she showed a cape, she chose the model, the accessories, and the atmosphere in which the garment was presented. Often, she also conceived the issue's theme. "Subject to the collaborative process with editors, art assistants, and artists, my personality was pervasive but not obtrusive."

As art director she transformed American illustration from a saccharine service to an expressive art. "I avoided illustration that was weighed down by cliché or convention, and encouraged that which was unique to the editorial context," Pineles said. She launched the illustration careers of the likes of Seymour Chwast and Robert Andrew Parker (whose work was then showing in art galleries) and commissioned illustration from painters Ben Shahn, Jacob Lawrence, Kuniyoshi, Raphael Soyer, and Robert Gwathmey. She was convinced that the magazine's audience of teenage girls was intelligent enough to appreciate sophisticated art, and so she gave her artists unprecedented freedom. The convention in the late 1940s and 1950s was for art directors to give the illustrator rather detailed instructions of what passage or sentence to illustrate. Rather than force her artists to mimic the text, Pineles allowed them to paint what they felt. "If it was good enough for their gallery, then it was good enough for me," she explained. The artists also made her design differently. "My sense of magazine pacing was altered because I had to separate one artist from another by distinctly different stories. And I was forced to use different typography than I had been used to so as not to compete with the illustration."

Her photographic sense was equally unconventional. Pineles found fashion to be a fascinating subject, and was interested in the effect it had on the way people felt about themselves. But she despised the haughtiness of *Vogue*'s fashion photography and urged *Seventeen*'s photographers to focus on real-life situations. "Make the models look normal," she charged.

Type was as important as image. Pineles developed sound typographic principles on which *Seventeen* was based. "Changing the typeface for the headlines or the body type were outside manifestations. Although they would make the reader think that the magazine had changed, but actually, in order to make substantial alterations the contents had to be tackled from the outset," she explained. Nothing was formulaic. Type was designed according to the same expressive mandates as illustration, and her layouts had a timeless quality.

As an art director, Pineles described herself as personally responsible for interpreting in visual terms the contents of a publication, from appointing photographers and artists to certain features, to deciding to use many typefaces or just one. "But most important is the talent to harness it and create momentum so that the reader will keep turning the pages."

# BASCOVE'S IMPACT ON ILLUSTRATION

I've been drawn to Bascove's imagery ever since I first laid eyes on her book covers and jackets designed in the early 1970s. Her intense, emotion-charged woodcut/pen and brush illustrations and gothic hand-crafted lettering grabbed the senses and stirred the imagination. The books with her unmistakable imprimatur were always found on the shelves of my favorite bookstore haunts where avid readers spent hours on end. It was hard to miss them.

Bascove was the go-to illustrator for various genres of serious and quirky fiction including Alice Walker's *Meridian*, Thomas Mann's *Black Swan*, Simenon's *Aunt Jeanne*, and the most disturbingly expressive in her oeuvre, the image of the self-cannibalistic prisoners on Mykhaylo Osadchy's *Cataract*. Over her illustration career, she has combined a range of graphic styles from film noir to German expressionist with a hint of surrealist mystery for good measure. Doing so, she personified a trend for symbolism and allegory in American illustration, a generational rejection of conventional literalism and passé romanticism. Her work transcended commercial norms, imposed new tropes and appealed to readers that could tell books by her covers.

From my first encounter with the artist with the intriguing monAnymic artist (full name Anne Bascove, b.1946) enduring a chance encounter when our mutual friend, John Baeder, introduced us outside her apartment building on University Place near Washington Square. I had been following her work with the plan of asking her to work for me on the *New York Times* op-ed page, but she was not a carbon copy of her melancholy pictures. I had pictured someone who was dark and brooding perhaps, as her work suggested. In fact, while serious about her art, she was not a depressive personality. First and foremost, she was the artist whose work was a combination of graphic linearity and soothing chromatic hues that was so perfectly suited to my penchant for early twentieth-century expressionistic and surreal imagery when, at that time I was art director of the *New York Times* op-ed page, after that meeting I began to give her work—and we've been friends for almost forty years.

In 1975, Bascove was among the first wave of new illustrators I relied upon to make my *Times* pages come alive—first on the op-ed page and then in the *Book Review*. Bascove's passion was for interpretation. She always loved doing book work, "but my imagery was too dark for some people," she told me in an interview for my 1986 book

*Innovators of American Illustration.* "I was literally told by publishers that if they had jobs needing a dark vision, which was rare, they'd rather give it to a man—a man, they said, has a family to support." Of course, that didn't stop her, and her work was eventually in great demand. Around twenty years ago, she abruptly stopped doing illustration and began seriously painting. It wasn't a great leap, in the formal sense, but for an illustrator to be taken seriously as a painter has never been easy.

# TRIUMPH OF WILL (BURTIN)

**D**espite a rise in the number of archives, exhibits, and monographs dedicated to the graphic and information designers who decades earlier had made impressive inroads in the field, it is surprising that there is a lack of knowledge about the collective professional design heritage. Many of design's legacy figures, whose accomplishments should be familiar to design students, professionals, and researchers, have slipped through the cracks because graphic design history is stalled. Suffice to say, there are many new kinds of histories that have yet to be explored.

Essential to the development of any foundational graphic and information design history, "form-givers" and "influencers" must be known by more than their names. Teams, movements, and schools must be contextualized within other political, cultural, and technological histories of their times. R. Roger Remington and Sheila Pontis's book is about one person who deserves a share of attention. Will Burtin's approach to visualization was "grounded in his lifelong career focus on combining convenience, clarity, usability, timeliness, [and] beauty." He began around the same time that Czech émigré designer Ladislav Sutnar introduced an archetypal information-heavy navigational system for industrial and product catalogs (for the Sweets Catalog Service), through distinct typographic hierarchies and easy-to-use grids, Burtin helped pioneer what has become known as information design in the sciences and technology, and in particular, devised advanced visual methods for clarifying otherwise densely presented theorems, postulates, and other intellectual platforms. As an art director for the magazines *Fortune* and *Scope* (the in-house periodical for the Upjohn pharmaceutical company) Burtin employed an artist's eye with a scientific fluency to create two- and three-dimensional graphics and typographic-based exhibitions that increased data fluency and popular comprehension of health care, finance, industry, and science. His most reputed work, a walk-through display of the human cell, introduced viewers to a magnified microscopic universe as a larger-than-life, unforgettable environment. This had a significant influence on designers entering this now-large discipline.

Born in 1908 in Cologne, Germany, Will Burtin apprenticed and became an exhibition and graphic designer during the postwar mid-1920s. Despite economic deprivations and political uncertainties stemming from military defeat, Germany's Weimar Republic experienced a brief period of economic growth that triggered a wave of progressive/modern *Gebrauchsgraphikers* (commercial artists). Art and culture were also reaching an apex of an avant-garde ascent. Experimentation spilled into commercial printing, advertising, graphic design, and typography. The 1920s was a great age for designers—and for Burtin.

For Burtin design was not just a service, it was a mission. Rooted in mathematically precise organization and artful aesthetics, he effortlessly thinned out the thickest data forests while spotlighting meaning. He made what the authors call "facts of the world" facilitate knowledge and its comprehension and inform action. Burtin believed that good design was a curative for the chaos of the cataclysmic European war. Remington and Portis re-create the unique systematic "process boxes" that Burtin used to structure his graphic outcomes. What distinguishes this book from many design monographs, aside from the specific case studies, is the publication for the first time of firsthand accounts of his ideas and theories. His earliest work involved design for industry, social welfare, and education. Modernity was influenced by new technologies that promised a better future—or the illusion of one. This is the bedrock on which Entwurfe Bürtin (Studio Burtin) built its reputation.

In 1938 Will and Hilde Burtin fled Germany for the United States where his innovations were enthusiastically embraced for his intellectual gift for imagining complex data in simplified visual forms.

This book by R. Roger Remington and Sheila Pontis, preceded in 2007 by Remington and Robert S. P. Fripp's splendid *Design and Science: The Life and World of Will Burtin*, dives even deeper into Burtin's essential role in visualizing science, which today is the cornerstone of a significant *information design practice* concerned with making science more accessible and revealing rarified information to a wider segment of the larger world.

# JANET FROELICH: THE ART DIRECTOR'S ART DIRECTOR

- - - - - - - - - - - - - - - - - - - - - - - - - - -

**T**he traits that make a great magazine art director are not always visible to the naked eye. Obsessive attention to detail is a fairly common one. Extreme interest in the content of the magazine distinguishes art directorial virtuosity from mere perfunctory professionalism. And then there's that elusive characteristic called "passion." The great art director must have it or what's the point? These contribute to being above and beyond, but are not the only ingredients.

Take Janet Froelich, for example. She is a great art director not simply because her magazines look and feel smart, which is to be expected. Her stature derives from more than passion for what she does; she is consumed by the art, design, typography, and photography that she does it with. To be a perfectionist—which she is—is one thing, to be an artist whose métier is perfection—which she also is—is the essence of great art direction.

Of course, "artist" is a slippery word. Art is a consequence, not an intention, of graphic design. Just because a magazine looks and feels good to the eye does not make it art. Nonetheless, Froelich's art is the printed page. She is a great art director because her artistry flows through her pages.

As a seasoned newspaper designer at the *New York Daily News*, Froelich joined the *New York Times*, where I worked as an art director for thirty-three years. She started as the deputy *Magazine* art director, eventually rising to art director and eventually design director (including *T-Style* fashion and design magazines) before leaving for her current post at *Real Simple*. Perhaps because she was not a formally trained graphic designer, she absorbed as much from those people she hired as they from her. During her *Times* tenure, she balanced the need to perpetually learn more craft with a keen understanding of the material and equally adept aesthetic sensitivity. Froelich saw the big picture of the magazine better than anyone else. Pacing was key to success and even with decreasing editorial well spans, she brought cinematic dynamism to the *Times Magazine*'s editorial well. She made a mark that still resonates.

Froelich inherited a magazine with a long tradition as the feature flagship of the "Grey Lady." In the 1950s and early '60s it was the sole "color" section of the

*New York Times*, the only element of the Sunday paper that was actually "designed" by someone other than a "make-up man," although it was very functional design. (Incidentally, it was also the section most treasured by teenage boys for its color women's underwear advertisements.) By the late 1960s Louis Silverstein, the first and only *Times* corporate art director, began making sophisticated typographic changes. Working with younger designers, the *Magazine*'s conceptual and visual components were soon on a par with other well-designed mass-market magazines. By the early 1970s, when Ruth Ansel was named its art director, the *Times Magazine* was a showcase for world-class photography and illustration. The typographic scheme also improved, and layouts were dramatic and memorable. Prior to the introduction of color in the *Times* news sections, the *Magazine* was a magnet for many Sunday readers.

A string of art directors, including Roger Black, Ken Kendrick, and Diana Laguardia, preceded Froelich. Each invested their respective design personalities; each introduced newly minted talented designers, typographers, illustrators, and photographers. Customized design was key to the *Magazine*'s success—it was part of yet distinctive within the larger *Times*. From the mid-1970s through Froelich's tenure in the early 2000s (and into the tenure of her successor, Arem Duplessis), the *Magazine* earned hundreds of well-deserved design industry awards, not just for its high-quality work, but for the surprises it routinely bestowed on its readership.

Art directing a magazine that does not have to sell on the newsstand has distinct benefits—including an unfettered cover "canvas," on which to experiment with image and form. This is something the *Times Magazine* is known for. The other plus is having the freedom to vary content within certain parameters. So despite its strict grid, the *Magazine*'s interiors are loose enough to adapt to the content of each issue. Froelich certainly enjoyed the strictures yet relished the freedoms as well. During her tenure at the *New York Times Magazine* (and later as design director for the *T-Style* magazines too), she retained a *Times* identity while pushing the perceptual limits of the magazine.

Doubtless there is a mandate to situate Froelich in the pantheon of women art directors—of which there are many more than one might expect. It is true that editorial design was until thirty years ago more or less male dominated, but women were not a minority (indeed Lillian Baseman and Ruth Ansel have already been recognized in this series). Women held the reins of many important magazines. Ansel was, herself, art director of the *Times Magazine* during the early to late 1970s. So, to segregate Froelich by virtue of gender is not an entirely fair assessment of her place in the art directorial pantheon.

If I were to write a novel or direct a film about a magazine art director—and not one where the art director is a supporting character under the thumb of some domineering editor—Froelich would be my model. Her boundless energy in the trenches, her ability to effectively argue with the most articulate wordsmiths over the efficacy of this photograph or that illustration, is the essence of how I view an art director. This is not to imply she is a stereotype. Froelich may share some characteristics with other creative types, but her manner is uniquely her own.

And what about style? Unlike some editorial art director-designers, Froelich does not impose one signature look to fit all. Favorite photographers? Yes. Illustrators? Yes. Even typefaces? No doubt. But the measure of her security is a freedom to transcend style and respond to content and context.

So, where is Froelich situated in the continuum of art direction as the tectonic plates of the field are moving? She is on terra firma as one who has made a major mark on the magazines she's guided and the profession she's led. In short, she's an art director's art director—and that is visible to anyone with eyes to see.

# HURRAH FOR MILTON GLASER

**A** decade before he died in 2020, Milton Glaser told me that this is his last hurrah. To which I said ha ha! At eighty-one he was still creating significant design at full capacity, and an exhibition, *In Search of the Miraculous or One Thing Leads to Another*, at the AIGA National Design Center in New York was the evidence. This exhibit, mounted as a celebration of Glaser's receiving the 2010 National Medal of Arts from President Barack Obama, is all recent work from the past decade. Rather than yet another career-defining retrospective (he's had those before), these conceptually paced "walls" of work "attempt to plot the path of a series of design ideas over a period of time to demonstrate how one influences another, and how any two ideas brought together can produce a totally new idea that cannot be anticipated," noted the AIGA website.

Glaser wanted to make this a unique experience, which not only displays his current wares but reveals how ongoing political, social, and spiritual concerns inform his work for clients and himself. In the accompanying "Users Guide" (a long accordion brochure) to the main and supplementary walls (the latter titled "The Client Didn't Get It," which speaks for itself), Glaser explains the underpinning of his recent design was when he studied kundalini yoga "with a guy named Rudi, who owned an Asian art gallery on Fourth Avenue in the East Village," he writes. "Kundalini yoga is all about releasing serpent energy that resides at the base of the spine." From this simple recollection the narrative transitions into a very brief explanation of his identity design in 2004 for the Rubin Museum of Art, and the series of silk screens, posters, and a gilded copper entry wall.

From this interest in Buddhism and yoga, he started producing posters influenced by Buddhist patterns, which in turn, lead to a commission from a swami and Tibetan rug company investor to design handmade rugs. His prints for Rubin, *Light Tantra* and *Dark Tantra* became full-sized rugs. These led to designing a carpet for the new School of Visual Arts Theatre on West 23rd Street (where Glaser was acting Chairman of the Board), which he was commissioned to redesign in 2008. Moving from Tibet to revolutionary Russia, he decided to base the Theatre's identity on Vladimir Tatlin's *Monument to the Third International*. He notes it had "long fascinated me, and I created a series of studies based on it." The logo he devised is a stylized version of an eighteen-foot, three-ton kinetic sculpture—a twenty-first-century Tatlin—that sits on top of the marquee and rotates every hour to address "the nature of time."

PEOPLE                                                                                          77

There was indeed a miraculous quality to the way Glaser's work segued so naturally from one project and form to another, while still addressing his clients' respective needs. Glaser's voice was clear, but not at the expense of the message. However, a very recent interest was more of a challenge. Drawn from his interest in Tibetan art and a personal "inquiry into the nature of perception," a section of the exhibition titled "Stumbling in the Dark" included prints and posters that are shades of black, devoid of contrast. "Does the difficulty of seeing these images . . . provoke the viewer to pay more attention," he asked. "Or does it produce indifference and irritation?"

Rather than exhibit a selection of faits accompli, Glaser uses this show as a narrative platform to address what he described as a perpetual sense of "doubt and confusion." Glaser's show changed the rules of critical engagement with "commercial art" through questions usually asked in the privacy of a studio. "Certainty," wrote Glaser, "is a closing of the mind. To create the new, requires doubt."

I doubt, however, that viewers will fail to find this exhibit incredibly illuminating. Hurrah! Hurrah!

# SEYMOUR CHWAST'S YEAR OF THE MASK

‐ ‐ ‐ ‐ ‐ ‐ ‐ ‐ ‐ ‐ ‐ ‐ ‐ ‐ ‐ ‐ ‐ ‐ ‐ ‐ ‐

**S**eymour Chwast was cofounder in 1954 of Push Pin Studios with Milton Glaser (who died on June 26, 2020). Comprised of an eclectic band of artists and designers, Push Pin was best known for its style of editorial and advertising illustrations, book and record covers, and package and typeface designs that transformed formulaic commercial art into distinct visual languages that were conceptually driven, sometimes decorative, occasionally abstract, frequently comical, and always expressively whimsical. This is also an apt description of Seymour himself.

With the pandemic lockdown in full force, I had not laid eyes on Chwast, who also happens to be my best friend and collaborator on over fifteen books, for almost a year (even on Zoom). He was as happy as anyone could be, riding out the storm, out of harm's way, ensconced in his spacious Northwest Connecticut studio overlooking the snowy winter and verdant spring foothills of the Berkshire Mountains. His quarantine hours were spent working on his many projects as a daily binge of vintage films perpetually played in the background, filling his rooms with iconic movie dialogue. It was veritable heaven on earth, you might say.

Obstinately productive, Chwast wrote and illustrated four new children's books, edited and designed an expansive monograph titled *Poster Man* of 120 greatest posters (published in Spring 2021), and completed a comically eccentric guide to human hell (scheduled for release in Fall 2021, lord willing), which includes some of the most exquisite satiric drawings he's ever done, in this case of every underworld known to man (I wrote the text). This profusion of genius was all made, just incidentally, prior to Chwast's turning ninety on August 17, 2021!

If you know Seymour like I do, it is not surprising he accomplished what he did or that this output was still not nearly enough to satisfy his insatiable need to make art. So, unbeknownst to me, while I was toiling on *HELL*, Seymour was having an earthly delight working on a series of new portrait paintings inspired by the flamboyant Mexican Luche Libre ("freestyle") wrestlers known for their brassy masks and superhero costumes that since the early twentieth century have been a defining peculiarity of Mexican popular culture.

How did he transition from children's picture books to *HELL* to Luche Libre? It may seem an odd juxtaposition, but it is in Chwast's nature to make the most out of a masked-up mass lockdown. Still, even I am amazed by how seamlessly he compartmentalizes.

I am certain, however, if the Luche Libre style did not already exist as an inspiration, Chwast would have invented it, because, as he explains: "Some of my favorite artists have done wonders exploiting facial forms: Picasso, Francis Bacon, Georges Rouault." And about these masks in particular he says: "I can explore visual ideas without losing the subject . . . just suggesting eyes, nose, and mouth. The mask raises questions. Does the mask hide the wrestler's fears? Does it give him an identity with character that he thinks he needs?"

Luche Libre masks may have inspired this series of eighty large canvases and still counting but there's more to it than pandemic kitsch or pop fashion: "I am not limited by them," rather "starting a painting with a mask idea gives me freedom I would not have with a totally abstract work."

Larga vida a la libertad!

# DIANE KEATON'S SAVED IMAGES

**66** **I** love your jacket," I told Diane Keaton, Oscar-winning actress, photographer, and author, during a recent telephone interview about her eclectic new book, *SAVED: My Picture World*, which dropped last Friday. I was allowed fifteen minutes for the interview and thought that maybe a compliment about the book might break the ice. Surprisingly, there was no ice to break. In fact, I felt like I was talking to Keaton's most iconic film character, Annie Hall (Keaton was born Diane Hall, by the way), and I was put at ease hearing her delightful Annie voice responding to my comment the way Annie might have said it: "Really?! No? Come on ... you mean you *really* like it?" I was waiting for her to use the word "neat."

I don't usually review photography books unless the content really grabs me. It's not because I'm anti-photo; I just don't possess a critical framework for judging the work. But I do know what I like, and Ms. Keaton's *SAVED* hits the right buttons, from its title to content—just the right balance of mystery, vernacular, personal history, and artistry. I also think her response to my compliment was genuine; even a veteran film personality would be insecure about another person's perception of such an intimate and personal book. The truth is, the book has a niche audience, of which I am a member.

The jacket signals the darkly comedic slant that fits Keaton's sensibilities. I love the bold typography and subtle pictorial gag—a droll photo by the late Milanese photographer Giuseppe Pino of an ornate but empty picture frame that is being held by three hands, not two. (The surprising third hand suggests the surrealistic undercurrent throughout the book.) The title *SAVED* is typeset in extra bold red sans serif caps above the image, which is printed to appear like a metal votive against the black matte background, with "BY DIANE KEATON" in red type underneath. The subtitle is saved for the title page.

*SAVED* is a hybrid art-as-life memoir told through images, paired with revealing brief essays that introduce the thirteen thematic sections, each with expressive typographic opening spreads designed by Ethel Seno. The sections feature a sampling of Keaton's favorite lost-and-found anonymous images, her personally snapped photos, as well as a trove of surreal photocollages, various scrapbook pages, and as the finale, a compelling section of abstract collages by Keaton's brother Randy Hall, who grew up with mental challenges and now suffers from dementia. The book is lovingly dedicated to him.

The first of the three sections represented graphically above is "The Ostentatious Flash," in which Keaton shot candid photos of ordinary folks on

Hollywood Boulevard with her trusty Rolleiflex and flash, surprising some, upsetting others. ("I remember taking shots of a particularly dapper older gentleman who spotted my flash and threw a bag of french fries at my head," she writes.) Next, of "Cut & Paste," Keaton says she and her siblings were avid collage makers. ("Our love for the picture world was much more appealing than the beach, TV, movies and even our family trips to Death Valley or Doheny Beach.") And finally, "Red" features Randy's work. ("Randy was a master of rearranging the female gender to suit his imagination.")

The book's thirteen sections are portfolios of ephemera and minutia that fit under the titles "The Brain That Wouldn't Die" (creepy vintage monster movie stills, like the one where a mad scientist keeps his beautiful fiancée's head and brain alive in a tray), "Teeth a Warning" (graphic photos from the 1930s *Clinical Diagnosis of Diseases of the Mouth*), "Pigeons of Trafalgar Square" (photos of "manic swooping down" and "willful plunges" of the aroused urban fowl), "Dogs" (pages from vintage scrapbooks of cutout pooches), "Light of Day" (portraits of survivors of automobile accident injuries), and more eclectic oddities drawn from photo archives and ephemera stashes Keaton told me she's been buying and long collecting, which she pins up on a thirty-to-fifty-foot mood wall in her home. "I love that wall," she said.

*SAVED* appeals to my love of quirk without reservation.

Many of her treasured objects and effigies were bought at swap meets (a.k.a. flea markets). She keeps her collecting life separate from her acting one—"acting is weird," she said with a hint of irony, given the weirdness that Keaton saved in *SAVED*—but if you picture the dinner scene in *Annie Hall* in which the Hall family discusses swap meets, the dialogue comes directly from the fact that Keaton and her sister Dorrie are addicted to buying crazy stuff at such gatherings.

One Sunday, decades ago, I caught sight of Keaton intently browsing at New York's now decimated 26th Street flea market. I told her that and she jokingly asked how she looked. I implied that in a long gray wool coat and scarf, she looked like the typical flea denizen, of which only a few have not gone digital.

I've collected many scrapbooks and personal ephemera collections and thought I was satiated, but *SAVED* shows me there's still more to marvel and enjoy. What a neat book to have.

# ELI KINCE INTRODUCED ME TO THE VISUAL PUN

I am indebted to the designer, design educator, and painter Eli Kince for providing a hallelujah awakening for me years ago in the way I think about graphic design. His long-out-of-print book *Visual Puns in Design: The Pun Used As a Communications Tool* revealed the quintessential tool of design ideation. Published one year before *A History of Graphic Design* by Philip B. Meggs, another revelatory volume, *Visual Puns* figured in how I write about design to this day.

Elvin Elias Lee Kince did not invent the visual pun in graphic design, yet his book defined the term and celebrated the method of conceiving visual ideas that had been used by artists and designers for ages. The verbal pun is unfairly called the lowest form of humor; however, Kince validated its prominence as the tool for creating high-level visual, typographic, and design ideas. For me, the book is a Rosetta Stone for understanding the theory and practice of the pun.

I do not believe that Kince received the recognition he deserved for writing *Visual Puns*. In addition to shining light on how dependent logo and other conceptual designers are on the pun, it was among the first analytical design books, which have since grown into a crowded publishing genre. I know of at least ten other books—including some of my own—that address visual puns as the foundation of contemporary design language, yet all roads lead back to Kince, whose place in design history has been sadly overlooked. So I sought him out to find out more about the book and his subsequent career as a designer and artist.

As design history is currently being reevaluated, Kince's contribution has even more relevance. So, I sought him through email to ask the follow questions. Why did he decide upon this theme for his Yale University design thesis? Brad Thompson, a master of the visual pun, wrote the foreword; was Thompson his inspiration? What was the process for getting this book published? I peppered Kince with so many questions his response was to write a veritable autobiography, which I take pride publishing verbatim:

I am not sure how to answer your email briefly. I guess I will start with the beginning of my college life.

It started the afternoon I was being consoled by a friend as we sat on a street-side curb in Cleveland, Ohio, one sun-drenched afternoon. I was distraught because a bottle of milk I had bought for my daughter had slipped out of its handle and broke. The Lawson store manager would not refund the money nor replace the product. He said that he believed that I drank the milk, and then I broke the strap to get a free bottle of milk. I did not have enough money to buy another bottle, and I was penny-less, and I felt worthless. I was on the verge of hopelessness, but I was trying to figure out how to provide for my daughter.

I remember sitting there, tears welling up in my eyes and feeling sorry for myself. Somehow, maybe due to traffic or a gust of wind, a sheet of wind-tossed paper flipped around the corner and skipped above the street surface toward us. As it started to dart past us, I reflexively and absentmindedly stamped on it—more of a distraction than a purposeful intent.

It turned out to be an advertisement for the Pell Grant. A government program that is usually awarded only to undergraduate students who displayed exceptional financial needs. My friend and I fit that description precisely at that time. We applied, and within five months, we received grants, and we decided to attend Bowling Green State University. It seemed that I was college-bound and bound to be the first in my family to go to college. It was so much better than the steel mill factory job option that I had initially accepted as my fate. I spent three years at BFSU [sic], where I majored in accounting. I remember that I wanted to study art-related subjects, but it was also clear that I had to support my daughter.

To help pay the bills, I used to draw portraits on the street, and I sold posters I made at performances of the singers and singing groups like Marvin Gaye, The O'Jays, the Four Tops, and others.

After I destroyed my middle finger on my left hand in a steel-and-die factory accident during my third year, I decided to transfer to the University of Cincinnati. I heard they had a work-study program that allowed students to work in their discipline for two semesters and go to school for two semesters. I thought that would be a safer way to support myself and my daughter and possibly find an art-related career.

I initially went to CU for the work-study in Interior Design, which I did for my first summer in Cincinnati.

But one day, toward the end of the summer, I saw students working with typography in the Commercial Arts Program. I was excited about what they were doing, and I applied to the program. Gordon Salchow, the department chair, interviewed me and my brown paper bag portfolio of drawings, posters, and photos of me drawing portraits in the streets. He accepted me into the program, which soon became known as Graphic Design.

Over the next four years, I learned a lot about designing from Gordon Salchow,

Inge Druckery, and others. And before I knew it, the final semester had arrived, and the question of "What's next?" came with it. I remember Gordon asking me what I was going to do once I graduated. I told him that I wanted to go to Switzerland to study under Matthew Carter and because I thought America was too racist toward Black people for me to get fair opportunities.

Salchow suggested I try applying to top American graduate schools first, and either way, I could still go to Switzerland later. He gave me the names of three prominent graduate school programs, and I sent out three graduate school program applications. However, once I received them, I immediately rejected one of the applications because the design was awful. I applied to the other two schools. The two remaining schools interviewed me and appeared interested in having me join their programs. One school offered me a full scholarship, room and board, and a financial stipend. They gave me one day, twenty-four hours, to accept their offer.

I remember asking the chair of the second school's design program his honest opinion on what I should do. He called Yale, and he said that the Yale Graduate Program told him that they put me on a "hold" list. I remember he took me for a stroll in the campus garden outside his office and advised me to hold out for Yale. He said I might even learn more from his school's program, but the name would serve me much more in the long run if I got into the Yale University program.

I took his advice and held out for Yale, and then I waited for months to find out if it was the right decision. I can still remember the explosive relief of stress and energy when I opened the letter and read the great news that Yale accepted me into the master's program.

Now that I was in the program, the old familiar challenge piped up. How was I going to pay for my college expenses? I was able to get some financial aid, and eventually, I worked out a deal to do work for the university. I created posters for the fire marshal, such as the "crawl" posters. I also created dining hall posters for the food services during this period.

During my second semester, Paul Rand recommended me for the IBM office in San Jose, California, during the summer months between the first and second year at Yale. Some of the work I did while I was at IBM was the brand for "Quarter-Century Club" annual dinner announcement and the "construction site" and the "Back-at-Work" posters.

During my second year at Yale, I spent months of work on my thesis on the US highway signage system before Alvin Eisenman, the department chair, said he thought I was too pragmatic. He said that he was concerned that my thesis would lock me into a particular and limited career path. He suggested that we review my portfolio to see if we could find another option or direction on my work.

We noticed that I used a lot of play in my solutions, and we decided that I should pursue analyzing why I had been doing humor and play in my previous design work.

This direction became more and more exciting to me as I looked into humor and play in literature, fine arts, and graphic design throughout history. I was blessed to have magnificent professors who inspired me beyond dreams that I never dared to have before that time. They were brilliant, concerned, articulate, and dedicated to creating great designs and supporting the growth of their students.

I was impressed with and excited by Bradbury Thompson's print work and book designs, Paul Rand's RCA Morse code ad and his IBM designs, Armin Hoffmann's William Tell poster, and more. I remember that I finally learned how to "see" during a simple typography project with Dorothea Hoffmann. This vastly improved optical ability allowed me to break down what I saw into verbal concepts visually.

It was like, all of a sudden, I kept finding hidden jewels on full public display, in book covers, posters, and logomarks, shouting "look at me!", "what about me?" forcing me to review and analyze them and their communication mode. I remember falling in love, over and over again, with so many images.

During my research of various forms of humor, including literary, I observed a correlation between verbal puns and the work that I was naturally drawn to and creating. I noticed that I was attracted to work that was visual and meaningfully manipulative.

Eventually, I was able to separate the visual work into categories much like verbal puns.

I established the works as Visual Puns and sought to explain how and why they worked as puns.

The publishing of my thesis was encouraged by James Craig, a mentor who worked at Watson-Guptill. I pitched the idea, and they accepted it. I was assigned an editor to work with, Susan Davis, who was a tremendous help and guidance in getting written approvals of the images for the book. I codesigned the book with Bob Fillie, and Watson-Guptill did the rest. I often thought about doing a second edition, especially after the book slowly started receiving comments and mentioning in various writings, articles, and books.

# JERRY PINKNEY SAID "DRAW WHAT YOU KNOW"

— — — — — — — — — — — — — — — — — — — —

"**W**rite what you know," the standard creative writing workshop mantra, applies just as much to illustrators as to writers these days. In this age of merging media, it is essential for artists to "Draw what you know"— and what you'd like to know, and what you'd like others to know too. Don't keep it pent up. Everyone likes a good story. And every illustrator has a good story to tell—personal or otherwise. Sometimes these tales are conveyed through pictures alone, other times through word and image. And if the illustrator cannot write (since many become visual artists because they cannot or, more to the point, are afraid to write), then that is why a higher power created collaborators and editors.

Let's turn back the clock. Once upon a time, illustrators were primarily illuminators of authors' texts (they weren't slaves per se, but they were nevertheless indentured to the word). Cartoonists, however, were considered independent thinkers who translated thoughts into word and image. Cartoonists made statements; illustrators mimicked or interpreted. Although the constraint did not stop them from exhibiting a visual personality, nonetheless they often lacked a literary voice. Fast-forward to today: These traditional boundaries have long since blurred, and today drawing is, well, *writing* with pictures—a verbal-visual language that speaks to young and old with much the same complexity as text-alone narratives.

Children's books and comics have long been the primary venues for the marriage of these talents. In fact, with rare exceptions, children's books were the sole outlet. Now, with the inception in the 1980s of the publishing genre of "graphic novels," illustrators (and cartoonists and comics artists and, for that matter, painters and photographers) have found another means to convey stories, the themes of which have exponentially expanded to include very complex material, not the least including illustrative autobiography, memoir, and a hybrid of the two. Writing and drawing "what you know" is practiced more vociferously than ever—revealing more intimate revelations and more.

Autobiographical works are variously conceived for different effects. Some are transcriptions from distinct memories of the past and present. Others probe into hazy or mysterious historical pasts. These demand in-depth research that often uncovers incredible secrets. *Maus* by Art Spiegelman, for example, the comic that arguably launched the graphic novel genre, was a labor of emotional discovery. The protagonists, Spiegelman's parents depicted as mice, victims of Nazi (cats) persecution and ultimately survivors of the Holocaust, are presented in this form only after intense exploration. The anthropomorphic conceit was a means for Spiegelman to both attach and detach from the pain that he lived through as a child of survivors (in fact, his mother had committed suicide when he was in college, and his father grieved until his death). Yet after years of relentless interrogation, a narrative emerged that formally combined the language of comics and children's books and was as historically accurate as possible.

The Holocaust, which was once a taboo subject for children's books, was initially considered a callous—even tasteless—theme for comic books. But when presented as autobiography through the voices of those who endured it, critical resistance to the book evaporated. Before *Maus*, *Barefoot Gen*, a Japanese manga by Keiji Nakazawa, about a six-year-old boy who survives the atomic blast in Hiroshima, tackled equally difficult material combining first-person narrative with historical documentation. As the first Japanese manga to be translated in the United States, it doubtless inspired the wave of autobiography and memoir to follow. Children's books have circuitously benefited from the increased thematic range of graphic novels, if not as memoir per se, as stories drawn from real life that was heretofore taboo.

I don't actually recall reading any comic or children's books drawn from intimate autobiography when I grew up in the 1950s in New York City. Most of my books were fairy tales and benign animal stories with banal images. Other than those ubiquitous Classics Illustrateds, comic book adaptations of classic novels—and some of these, like *Three Years Before the Mast*, were fictional memoirs—children's literature stepped lightly if at all in this area. It is possible that such things existed, but either veiled behind layers of symbolism and allegory or kept away from my impressionable self. Of course, there were various biographies that were the official, myth-perpetuating hagiographies of famous people, but these do not count. Yet editorial attitudes began changing in the late 1960s, along with so much other turmoil in American society, when a new generation that gradually pushed the boundaries of appropriateness. Children's book author/illustrators took chances and entered an inner realm that was the precursor of the "draw what you know—and what you'd like to know" philosophy.

Jerry Pinkney appears to have adopted this concept early in his career. Although the majority of his books are not autobiographical in the conventional sense, the fact that he was African American in a white-dominated field—a field that ostensibly ignored the African American experience except as stereotyped folklore— provided an autobiographical imperative. "I wanted to show that an African American artist could make it in this country on a national level in the graphic arts," he once said. "I want to be a strong role model for my family and for other African Americans." Not only that, he sought to bring the classic tales of African Americans to the fore as integral components of the larger American culture. His author collaborators, notably Julius Lester, had the same mission. And Pinkney's impressionistic representational illustrations for the likes of "John Henry" and "The Last Tales of Uncle Remus" (both by

Lester) helped raise the perception of these folkways away from those Disney caricatures that fostered dubious racial archetypes.

Of the myriad stories Pinkney has illustrated, "Back Home" and "The Sunday Outing" by Gloria Jean Pinkney (his wife) suggest the most autobiographical resonance. Whether these are composites or direct recollections does not matter, the portrait, particularly in the latter book, of young Ernestine and her great-aunt Odessa, is a window to a distinctly loving family life that paints an alternative picture to the contemporary urban Black myths and attitudes of today. Pinkney captures the warmth of the family and the essence of the moment in time. And this can only be rooted in "draw what you know."

# PART 4:
# HERITAGE

# THE INFLUENCE OF NIGHTLIFE ON DESIGN

‑ ‑ ‑ ‑ ‑ ‑ ‑ ‑ ‑ ‑ ‑ ‑ ‑ ‑ ‑ ‑ ‑ ‑ ‑ ‑ ‑ ‑ ‑ ‑ ‑

**C**abarets, cafés, and nightclubs are as essential to the development of modern avant-garde art and design movements as are galleries, salons, and museums, perhaps more so. Every art and design movement from the late nineteenth through the twentieth and even twenty-first centuries had or have veritable laboratories in the form of bars, restaurants, theaters, whatever—where unfettered experimentation prospers or fails; and where all the arts come together into a fruitful, if anarchic, hodgepodge (think CBGB). This includes visual arts, literature, poetry, sound, music, dance, drama, and hybrids of them all. From this witch's brew, creative concoctions come to a boil.

The legendary haunts (many located in seedy locales) are where rebels mix and intermingle their respective arts. During the 1880s Parisian denizens founded le Chat Noir (the Black Cat) Café, in 1916 the Cabaret Voltaire in Zurich is where Dada was born, in the 1920s Harlem's famous Cotton Club, Smalls Paradise, and the many other off-the-tracks wellsprings of the Harlem Renaissance and its jazz pioneers emerged, and in the 1960s on a street in Teheran, Iran, Rasht 29, where an eponymous club combined Iranian tradition with Western modernism. There are many more.

The histories of these characteristically unorthodox cabarets have been covered here and there, but just this week an extensive and impressive volume devoted to these famous (and infamous) locales is now published in the United States. Titled *Into The Night: Cabarets and Clubs in Modern Art* edited by Florence Ostende and Lotte Johnson, curators of the eponymous exhibition at the Barbican Art Gallery in London, links the respective clubs and argues that in their day (mostly 1920s and 1930s, although the book enters the late twentieth century too) this web of creative activity was comparable to the internet, with many of the clubs connected at least through the journals, magazines, and newsletters that contained social, political, and aesthetic manifestos that were shared among many.

Mostly edgy (my word not theirs) were performance spaces, all founts of new graphic, costume, interior design, architecture, and photography. In dance, Loie Fuller's "groundbreaking experiments with costume, light and movement were captured by Henri de Toulouse-Lautrec" in a series of lithographs. Stephane Mallarmé, himself an alternative symbolist poet, wrote that Fuller's performances were "at once an artistic intoxication and an industrial achievement." What a great way to describe modernity: "artistic intoxication and an industrial achievement." This represents a small part of the coalescing powers of performative art to bring all the cultural activities together in common cause—making art of the present and future.

Certain cabarets are so iconic that we all have at least heard of them. In Vienna Cabaret Fledermaus (The Bat) was conceived by the Weiner Werkstätte designer Josef Hoffman and graphiste (typographer and letterer and posterist) Kolo Moser. It has become one of the signature monuments of this 1907 movement (today the Neue Galerie in New York has replicated the aura of this cabaret for its own restaurant). In London, Frida Strindberg's Cabaret Theatre Club was billed as the first artists' cabaret in England and in addition to theatrics it was ground zero for Vorticist art and design. Zurich's Cabaret Voltaire in 1916 published an eponymous journal edited by Hugo Ball and cover designed by Hans Arp, which broke the ground for Dada graphic design experimentation in Switzerland and Germany. In Rome the Italian Futurists performed at Cabaret del Diavolo, for which Fortunato Depero rendered its devil "mascot."

For many who only know about cabaret from the musical film of the same name, this book will be a revelation to know that the cabaret, café, and club phenomenon was so widespread. I did not know that Café de Nadie (Nobody's Café, "so named because it always seemed empty") was home for a Mexico City avant-garde, the movement known as Estridentista.

Many artists that I've admired from Germany between the wars were involved with different nightlife dens. Schall un Rauch (Sound and Smoke) founded by dramatist Max Reinhard, issued a series of festschrift programs with designs by Hanah Hoch, Otto Dix, and others (I bought a fine facsimile in East Germany during the late 1980s). Painters like Karl Hofer and the splendid crayon and watercolorist Jeanne Mammen, who captured Berlin's underbelly for *Simplicissimus* and *Jugend* among other contemporary magazines, were integral players in performative arts.

Harlem had long had a vibrant arts scene at the turn of the century onward. By the 1920s two-thirds of New York's African American population lived there. So, it was no surprise that its nightclubs, jazz dens, and cabarets (presumably taboo for white visitation) was a high-powered magnet for New Yorkers of all races.

There was quite a lot of cross instigation and pollination that is well represented in an essay "The Walls Seem to Dance: Mapping the Connections between Cabarets and Clubs in Modern Art" by Lotte Johnson—she addresses such influences as Mexico City on Zurich and Paris and Rome or Paris, Vienna and Zurich. And most interesting are the Harlem artists' connections to the Nigerian Ibadan and Osogbo movements (in the 1960s).

*Into The Night: Cabarets and Clubs in Modern Art* is the catalog for the exhibition of the same name at London's Barbican Gallery, on view until January 19. I hope it will travel to the United States. We all know the influence that club culture and alternative performance space has on creative people in this country, but we tend to live in our respective moments, without seeing the larger picture. *Into The Night: Cabarets and Clubs in Modern Art* is a big book that covers between covers among the most significant of works done in, around, with, and for these wells of culture. At a time when many richly researched tomes are liberally produced on all manner of twentieth-century avant-garde art and design, this is on my forever list as one of the best.

# COMMAND RECORDS DESIGN HIT THE HIGH NOTES

— — — — — — — — — — — — — — — — — — —

I n 1939, the year that graphic designer, art director, and record cover pioneer Alex Steinweiss created the first original record album cover design for Columbia Records, *Newsweek* reported an increase in the sales of shellac 78 rpm discs to the tune of an 800 percent increase. Before this, records limited to six- or seven-minute durations per side were fitted into craft paper sleeves, bound into an actual "album" with the title embossed on the spine. They were displayed spine-out in music stores in a manner called "tombstones." Why it took so long to discover that using artwork was a better marketing strategy is anybody's guess. There were precedents, of course: Illustrated film posters induced audiences to buy tickets; illustrated sheet music covers were more seductive; and illustrated dust jackets teased potential readers into acquiring books, although the custom was to discard them once they were shelved at home. Records were, in fact, advertised through pictorial cardboard, easel-back countertop displays.

Yet self-contained advertising was more impactful. Album cover design hinted at the feelings, moods, and styles imparted by the recorded music. It added visual allure to the overall listening (and seeing) experience, and because they also protected records from damage, album covers had indefinite shelf lives.

Album covers had pride of place in the commercial design world too. Initially they were a tabula rasa, empty canvases that were less prescribed by constricting marketing rules and industry taboos than were other kinds of consumer packaging. There were myriad styles of illustration and typography as varied as the sounds emanating from the discs themselves. Also specific visual cues were created through graphic tropes to help the consumer distinguish classical from pop from avant-garde from spoken word, etc. While the quality of art and design did not always directly drive record purchases, if a particular piece of music hit the right chord, its illustrated album cover would invariably become iconic too.

By 1948 with the advent of the music industry's standard microgroove plastic twelve-inch 33⅓ vinyl LPs, cover art was perhaps more essential than before. One reason was that record stores large and small began to open all over the United States, leading to a growing industry. As new labels entered this competitive marketplace, musical genres demanded more aggressive marketing. Record containers were art directed to reflect the range of music and the popularity of musicians. Even before the 1950s, jazz and other experimental genres were starting to hit high notes and topped the charts with such labels as Blue Note, Paramount, Westminster, Verve, Prestige and Riverside Records, among others. Many of these labels were as hip for their art and design as for their sonic grooves.

One of the era's most prodigious labels, Command Records, founded in 1959 by bandleader and recording engineer extraordinaire Enoch Light (1905–1978) and George Schwager, made innovative sounds come alive through the tireless development of stereophonic exactitude. Producing their brand of progressive percussive, rhythmic string, and big band jazz music, Command aimed at "discriminating people who desire the finest in sound." They recorded such talents as Tony Mottola, Count Basie, Dick Hyman, Buddy DeFranco, the Ray Charles Singers, and Light's own Light Brigade. But Command's most significant contribution was its "painstaking research into all phases of the recording field," states the standard liner note on most of Command's albums, along with the "pledge that they will produce only recordings which will contribute to your musical enjoyment and successfully meet your high quality standards." Command accomplished their goals through sound fidelity that could only be achieved with multiple microphone pickup: "From the origin of the sound in a large acoustically perfect studio to the editing and re-recording to the final pressing of the record only the finest equipment is used." This was, after all, the hi-fi age.

Command was originally called Command Performance Records and later became Command ABC-Paramount with offices in the Paramount building on Times Square. It was produced largely with the devout audiophile in mind. Although it is not as famous today as, say, Blue Note, it is nonetheless as significant for its graphic design, a stunning mixture of mid-century modern typography and abstract graphic art.

Pictorial abstraction was a visual corollary to the improvisational music that was emerging from Command Records' studios. How deeply involved Light or Schwager were in the selection of cover artists is unclear, but they obviously preferred an abstract approach and trusted the designer and painter Charles E. Murphy (1933–2005) to design many of them on his own and be art director for a host of other well-known designers on a variety of jazz, easy listening, classical, and pop releases. Murphy, with a penchant for modern art, color theory, and jazz, studied at Yale School of Art and Architecture and was taught by the Bauhausian painter and color theorist Josef Albers. Murphy maintained his old school ties when he later commissioned Albers for the covers of the *Persuasive Percussion and Provocative Percussion* series, on which he employed purely nonrepresentational yet extremely provocative geometric forms. These were arguably Albers's only commercial assignments in the United States.

Murphy was more versatile than his former teacher. While also fond of abstraction, his collages and drawings were more representational (see *The Persuasive Trombone of Urbie Green Vol 2*) and he often played with typefaces in a demonstratively illustrative manner (see *Bongos Bongos Bongos* and *The Urbie Green 6-Tet*). He further injected some witty elements seemingly influenced by the likes of Paul Klee (see *Fabulous*). His approach to pure and symbolic geometry and playful linearity became the basis for Command's visual identity, which also included the abstract expression of George Giusti, one of Murphy's close friends, and S. Neil Fujita, who were also known as mid-century modernists and for designing dozens of book jackets and covers. Giusti also took this opportunity to experiment with drawing and collage.

Today the Command covers exude a contemporary sensibility yet also underscore a curiously bygone design aesthetic. Indeed, not everyone at the time was as smitten by the graphic direction as I am. The veteran modernist designer and teacher of graphic design history Lou Danziger told me: "Of course I saw the work which I generally did not care for [because] many look like design school exercises." Yet as a company vision they, at least, hold together.

Whether or not they were perceived as more style over substance at the time of their creation, today Command Records covers are striking for the graphic and branding power of the abstract format. They are also vividly identifiable not only because of Command's mnemonic script logo that sits usually in the right-hand corner, but for another key characteristic: All images were printed against a white background. Now that's good art direction.

# THE REVOLUTION WILL BE COMPUTERIZED

I mages of the future, as visualized on science fiction magazine covers, television and in films, triggered paroxysms of anticipation in many people like me. Computers were the cornerstone of this future, yet in the early years of the computer revolution the visual delight never quite matched the physical reality. After all, a computer is ostensibly a nondescript machine, and the advertisements for computers were equally conventional.

The sexiest computer advertisement I have ever seen was actually not an advertisement for a computer but rather about a computer—well, kind of what we've come to know as a computer: the famous film poster for Fritz Lang's 1927 dystopian science fiction masterpiece *Metropolis* that prominently features an arresting graphic of the *Maschinenmensch* ("machine-person" or robot), a shiny metallic automaton shaped like a woman.

*Maschinenmensch* is the archetype for (and the most familiar image of) all the movie androids that followed—yet what is most important is that the *Maschinenmensch* is by any other name a computer. Prior to the early 1960s and the first computer revolution (we're in the fourth now), robots (from the Czech word *robata* for forced labor) were not touted as computers per se but rather as fictional mechanical humanoid devices. Real computers in their early modern incarnation were, conversely, those behemoth mainframe "big brains" decked out with blinking lights, dials, perpetually rotating reels of magnetic tape, and complex circuitry that were housed in large temperature-controlled rooms and required several people to operate (not quite the Siri or Alexa of today). These machines were not like robots, which were the stuff of imagination, they were big metal boxes with keyboards.

But they were the future even if the ad styles used to sell and promote them were not inventive. Advertising creatives avoided using metaphor and allegory lest they romanticize, mythologize, and in the process of doing so, trivialize them. The businesses targeted by the ads saw their futures in terms of serious functionality.

If humanizing computers served as a tool for actually selling computer products, it was not through advertising campaigns. Instead, our visions of the computer came through fiction: motion pictures and TV shows featuring robots, like the *Maschinenmensch*, *Forbidden Planet*'s Robbie, *Star Wars*' C-3PO, *2001: A Space Odyssey*'s HAL, the TV series *My Living Doll*'s AF 709 (played by Julie Newmar), and other entertaining artificial intelligence apparati that fantastically (and at times presciently) bridged the gap between people and machines.

In fact, computers were welcomed with both enthusiasm and trepidation as personified in the 1957 Spencer Tracy–Katharine Hepburn romantic comedy film *Desk Set*, in which the employees of the fictional Federal Broadcasting Network research department (fact-filled human search engines), were worried to death that the EMERAC (Electromagnetic Memory and Research Arithmetical Calculator) mainframe would replace them at their jobs; it was, in truth, a justifiable fear. When businesses computerized and automated, they would indeed replace human beings. Disquiet always accompanies radical change. Whether or not imbuing computers with human characteristics made them more acceptable is debatable, but probably giving these powerful machines names and personalities did make them a little less intimidating (or what is now called user-friendly).

Purchasing computers was a huge investment, so selling them was a major challenge for advertising agencies and promotion departments charged with the task. As the business machine field evolved from producing analog calculating machines to mainframes (a.k.a. "big iron") for voluminous data processing, the various computer companies were more dependent on strong brand strategies and design to help earn their own recognition and success. The images of computers as time-savers and problem-solvers leading to profit generators were key assets in ad campaigns. As machines developed with increased computing power, the graphics and jargon used to describe these virtues broadened and grew. Yet while computer ads implied "we've-seen-the-future-and-it-is-us," there was nonetheless some technophobia to overcome too—from taking *our* jobs away to something much worse, ruling our lives.

Pop culture contributed (and continues) to our ambivalence with computers. One of the most disturbing (though entertaining) of the *Twilight Zone* episodes related to computers, "The Old Man in the Cave," addressed the vexing problem of ceding humans' control to machines. The plot revolves around an unseen yet ominous figure that governs the lives of a handful of survivors in a small postapocalyptic American town in 1974, ten years after nuclear bombs destroyed most of the earth. The eponymous old man in the cave determined the rules that the townspeople had to follow in order to survive. The messages came through a town elder, who interpreted the orders (i.e., not to eat the contaminated canned food that was stored in the town). When, owing to an existential crisis, the townsfolk discovered that the old man was actually a big computer hidden in the cave, they angrily rose up as a mob, destroyed it, rejected the old man's orders, and promptly died from consuming the radioactive food. As they died, they realized how much they owed to this digital *god* but resented it anyway and paid the price.

Yet in addition to the wave of anxiety over machines, there was also a sense of amazement and anticipation for the future attached to the computer that dated back to its early nineteenth-century origins. A century before the first computer revolution, the first machine to be described as a computer, the "analytical engine," was invented by a wealthy English "gentleman scientist," Charles Babbage. An offspring of the Industrial Revolution and great-grandfather of steampunk (a style that combines contemporary high technology with vintage Victorian veneers), the analytical engine would ultimately alter how data would be created, stored, and consumed. In theory it predicted the modern computer, although in practice it had some mechanical kinks. Conceived in 1833, the "engine" incorporated an arithmetic logic unit and integrated memory, and was designed to tabulate logarithms and trigonometric functions. And there is more: it was the precursor to a fully program-controlled, automatic mechanical, digital computing device, able to perform any calculation and store the material as well. The story gets better: Babbage worked closely with Augusta Ada King, the Countess of Lovelace, daughter of Lord Byron and a genius mathematician who published the first algorithm. She is dubbed both the pioneer of computer programming and a philosopher regarding the relationship of society to technology.

Computers have been around for ages, but advertising for them is only seventy years old. What would the advertisements for the "engine" have looked like? Visions of the future are always skewed toward what we already understand. The twentieth-century modern industrial and product designer Raymond Loewy, used the term MAYA (most advanced yet acceptable) to indicate how far forward an unprecedented concept can go before testing an average person's capacity to comprehend or appreciate its newness. This is why most advertising rarely strays too far from a recognized norm.

The majority of examples in this book—from trade magazines and professional technology publications aimed directly to corporate customers and only later toward everyday consumers—span a curious range of approaches, especially compared to other advertising genres between the 1950s and '90s. Unlike automobile ads, computer promos do not emphasize the status and beauty of the machine itself. Unlike food there is no focus on mouthwatering imagery or appetite appeal. Unlike pharmaceuticals there is not much allegory or metaphor used to depict the psychology behind the machinery.

Not all the ads from this period are decidedly banal. UNIVAC's "Electronics" shows an engagingly colorful, surreal planetary landscape with the atomic symbol in the center of the image circling the sun. And a black-and-white IBM ad shows a startling artist's conception of a satellite hovering over Earth over the title "New Moon." Although the advertisements were handled by an agency, IBM's graphic identity, overseen by corporate design consultants Eliot Noyes and Paul Rand, always gave priority to design, allowing abstraction to be part of the visual vocabulary.

As the computer systems expanded to include data storage banks, punch card readers, and data input and control stations, many of the illustrated ads showed an increased amount of the hardware operated by men in suits or women controlling huge apparatuses (see National Post-Tronic). When the 1950s came to an end, the advertisements gradually became a little more abstract as well. This was a time when NASA's space program was in full tilt, which would have been impossible without the aid of computers. Computers used in space travel were the focal point in many ads. Advertising took advantage of scientific discoveries to shift away from a business focus to the space age.

The most mold-breaking shift in computer promotion is an IBM ad headlined: "On April 7, 1964 the entire concept of computers changed." It was no exaggeration either: the ad showed a tight close-up of two fingers holding a tiny computer chip. This began the miniaturization of computers leading to the desktop computer represented by the Computer Terminal Corporation ad for the Datapoint 3300 screen/keyboard. Although it did not mark the end of ads showing multiple large mainframe components, it was the veering away from formulaic advertising into a more artful space.

When the "personal" computers were introduced in the late 1970s the average person came much closer to having access to their own machines (and destinies). Microsoft was founded, the first Apple was crudely built, and the act of "word processing" entered our consciousness. The advertisements shifted from solely targeting business and government and opened its doors to the public. However, mundane product photography and ham-handed typography did not do the products justice. Conceptually speaking, the TEC Model 70 product against a photo of lightning storm had little charm and less allure. If you assumed that when the 1980s rolled around, that new personal devices—significantly the first Macintosh computer in 1984 and various incredible applications, including video games, made it seem that advertising would become more sophisticated out of necessity, you'd be wrong.

From a design perspective, ads like those for MegaSoft and Atari were garish and loud, echoing the primitive pixelated interfaces that were the state of the art at the time. The future, at least technologically speaking, when seen through the lens of these advertisements, was not as exciting as one might have hoped. TV advertising was decidedly more creative in the 1990s. Steve Jobs and Jonathan Ive (1992 to be exact) began improving the product design for Apple, which influenced a new graphic design (packaging and advertisement) elegance. The quality of the graphic and advertising design during the 1990s at companies other than Apple and IBM continued to be a mixed bag of horsey and lovely. Apple changed the standard for advertising and design of products as well as stores, packaging, and hardware. Computers are so beautifully integrated into our lives, selling them as design objects may not be an issue.

# THE UNDER-APPRECIATED ART OF SUPERMARKET PACKAGING

I n design jargon, "appetite appeal" describes the level of sensory stimulation that a food package should have in order to attract consumers. A product covered with only type is by default less mouthwatering than one with photographs of a delicious chicken taco or cheese pizza.

But for brands, elegant typography and bold design can telegraph its own appetizing message. For upscale chains like Trader Joe's and Whole Foods, getting customers to keep coming back is about more than just hunger: Food packaging has to signal reliability, trustworthiness, and consistency. Different companies might want to emphasize different qualities in their products—Trader Joe's, for example, might want to signal its quirky personality, while the New York–based mini chain Fairway might emphasize value for money. But for every single product, design has to consider a wealth of different factors in order to best sell and market its products, and on the whole, American stores are considerably less creative and inspired than their European counterparts.

First things first: shoppers aren't at the store for beautifully designed labels. They're there for food. So price is often the most important factor, particularly for staples, such as milk, butter, eggs, and cereal. Other than a design snob, who really cares whether or not Trader Joe's generic Bran Flakes box looks like the national brand as long as the product is cheaper? And does it really matter that Fairway's "Golden Honey" plastic bear is a cloned copy of the more expensive original Dutch Gold Honey? But good design is good business. Supermarket "private labels" don't have to be bland, and there are reasons, aside from aesthetic pleasure, why a little improvement can go a long way. A package contains more than a product—it's a reliquary, of sorts, of that product's story (even its fabricated story), which can be a powerful selling tool. Scores of memorable brands have iconic packaging, such as Heinz, Coca-Cola, and Kraft.

Companies use bottles and labels to represent their respective reputations, which gives customers a certain pride of purchase and helps maintain the products' market superiority.

There is also a trend among certain independent brands to increase their footholds in competitive markets on the theory that new product plus striking design will be the tipping point. The unfettered, elegant packages for Siggi's yogurt, Sarabeth's jams, and Fizzy Lizzy beverages, if not iconic, have contributed to a pride of purchase among a growing number of loyal customers.

In 1998 I co-authored *Food Wrap*, a survey of new design styles and techniques for supermarket and specialty stores worldwide. The aim in doing the book was to prove that food packaging was not entirely dictated by long-followed design conventions but by more fashionable and personal typography and illustration. In the late 1980s, an increasing number of independent graphic-design studios were taking commissions away from traditional packaging design firms to create a new genre of premium products for a growing yuppie market. Then, during the 1990s a supermarket revolution of sorts took place, with stores undergoing modern redesigns and new upstart products becoming more visible in renovated aisles. Graphic designers found new ways to trigger consumers' Pavlovian responses through more nuanced typography, illustration, and color. The result was a dichotomy between mass-market and upscale products, with audiences often willing to pay more for food products that were designed with more sophistication.

While traditional supermarket brands are designed with straightforward imagery (a ripe tomato says tomato sauce) and stylized marquee logos, designs for the "fancy food" market are subtler in terms of logo, color, typography, and imagery. But in recent years, the line between the two sectors has blurred, with upscale design conceits being introduced to mainstream products.

No one does it better than the British chain Marks & Spencer on its Simply Food collection. Focusing on a young, middle class, fashion-conscious audience, Charlotte Raphael-Graham, head of Graphic Packaging at M&S, has created a veritable culinary boutique of consistently beautiful and imaginative display-worthy packages featuring hundreds of products, from eggs to orange juice. The soothing colors, delightful illustrations, and vibrant typography, designed with wit, create a unified overall store identity and pleasing shopping experience.

In close second, the budget French chain Monoprix has a range of colorful, carnivalesque packaging designed by the French agency Havas City that busts supermarket conventions by using only bold sans serif typefaces in caps covering all sides of the containers—not a picture of a sandwich or soup in sight. When all the products are displayed on the shelves it is clear that a great design mind is at the helm. Havas has said that the design represents the "simplicity, humility but also the cheerfulness of everyday life."

The same can't be said for Fairway. Its Magic Marker–esque Fairway logo doesn't complement other typefaces well, and most of its house-brand products seem like the name has been tacked on anywhere as an afterthought. Although nothing is egregiously ugly, there is a graphic dissonance and brand disconnect between their specific products, rather than an overarching direction, as though the supplier of each item made their own packaging leaving an empty space for the Fairway logo.

The house design at Trader Joe's toes the line, and sometimes achieves excellence. But here too, inconsistency reigns. Some of its cookie and cracker boxes, for instance, are given a nostalgic nineteenth-century engraving pastiche that suggests something from an old general store and implies "artisanal" production. But TJ's canned and frozen foods, including chili, garbanzo beans, and tomatoes, retain the blandly generic supermarket look, customized only with the Trader Joe's logo. More attention to the overall graphic design may not influence some customers, but for those attuned to such things it can make all the difference between loyalty and not.

Only Whole Foods, which created a sophisticated yet simple "handcrafted" typographic style for its first store in Gowanus, Brooklyn, deliberately challenged all the rules of conventional supermarket packaging. Designed by Mucca in New York, the system is built solely on simple yet distinctive labels that are fixed to transparent bags and plastic containers. Rather than use a photograph, the actual product is its own illustration. And what further sets the packages apart from other premium products is how well they are integrated into a larger design system throughout the store. The entire environment exudes appetite appeal.

Critics of packaging debate that the best package is *no* package, suggesting a return to the old-fashioned ways of selling food in bulk from burlap bags and wooden barrels. But branded packaged goods are not going away just yet, and good design not only addresses sustainability issues but also make the increasingly stressful supermarket experience a little more enjoyable.

# VIVA MEXICO!
# VIVA GRAPHIC
# DESIGN!

A fter four years of Donald Trump's vicious anti-Mexican jingoism, it is a welcome relief to refocus my attention on the Mexico known for its prolific output and abundant heritage of modern art on a par with the early twentieth-century Europe and mid-century United States. This Mexico also inspired an impressive legacy of political and social (and socialist) graphic commentary and the progressive periodicals (*revistas*) that published them; the Mexico that produced a wealth of printed material that can stand beside any of the innovative graphic design and typography from the past. From a treasure trove of the Mexican avant-gardes that are exhaustively chronicled in the 2010 book and exhibition *México Ilustrado: Libros, Revistas y Carteles 1920–1950*, to a wellspring of quotidian magazines, newspapers, and travel and tourist books, many designed with swagger and flair, Mexico is only now receiving its overdue share of exposure in art and design histories. And with this book, *Mexico The Land of Charm*, much of the nation's otherwise ephemeral graphic, photographic, typographic "applied art" is finally receiving the attention it deserves—because this book proves that Mexico is an important link in the history of Western graphic design style and form.

As a child in New York during the mid-fifties, I was unwittingly introduced to Mexican popular culture through one piece of art, José Clemente Orozco's 1931 painting *Zapatistas*, showing a procession of Mexican peasant guerrillas going to their death during the *Revolución Mexicana*. A framed reproduction of the work hung for as long as I could remember over my father's boyhood bed in my grandparents' Bronx, New York, apartment. Having immigrated to the United States from Eastern Europe around 1915, to my knowledge my grandparents had never set foot or even considered visiting Mexico. They were probably indifferent to the Mexican revolution that this painting so emotionally depicts. It may have been left behind by an earlier tenant, during a time when Mexico was one of many wellsprings of avant-garde art. But neither my grandparents nor my father ever explained the meaning of the picture to me or why it was randomly hanging in a child's bedroom—and I never asked why. However, I was mesmerized by the expressionistic solemnity of the peasants "as stiff," to quote a review in the *New York Times* "as the machetes they carry, locked in a grim forced march."

Orozco's somber imagery haunted me as child, yet later, as a young adult, it inspired me too. Mexican art or political history was far removed from my sphere of consciousness—frankly I had not even tasted Mexican cooking until I was in my early twenties. The little I did know about the history of America's southern neighbor initially came through popular movies like Elia Kazan's 1952 biopic *Viva Zapata* starring Marlon Brandon as the iconic peasant rebel leader and John Wayne's 1960 *The Alamo* starring Wayne as the American folk hero Davy Crockett, who fought and died for Texas's independence from the Mexican empire. As I got older, however, an interest in Mexican revolutionary culture captured my attention particularly through a growing awareness of the great Mexican muralists Orozco, Diego Rivera, and David Alfaro Siqueiros (the big three). I also learned about the profound number of cultural and political periodicals published in Mexico City and began to collect a few as part of a more inclusive collection. I had a particular fondness for newspapers and magazines as the activist medium of choice.

During the late 1960s, I was deeply involved in American "underground" left-wing publishing as an editor, designer, and illustrator. Earlier in the century, from 1910 to 1920, Mexico had been transformed by revolution where artists played a major role in their revolutionary culture; in the 1960s this was mirrored in US counterculture. In fact, the Mexican cartoonist who most piqued my interest—and with whom I could personally identify—was the printer, publisher, and illustrator José Guadalupe Posada (1852–1913); he produced literally thousands of pre-revolutionary and revolutionary critical newspaper broadsheets and pamphlets featuring comic woodcuts that satirized politics, religion, oligarchy, and social castes and customs. He rebelled against the exploitation of the poor of his day and conceived an iconic repertory of calaveras, human skulls and skeletons. These memento mori were inspired by the staple imagery from the Día de Muertos (Day of the Dead), and were used to project Posada's biting yet witty protests against government and clergy and class. Other than the vintage paper they were printed on, there was a certain timelessness to his satire, which contributed to why these cuts widely influenced young illustrators and cartoonists working for many mid-sixties North American underground papers. Posada's work was a combustible blend of playfulness and acerbity in manner that directly prefigured and influenced the American style of subversive comic strips of the anti–Vietnam War era.

In addition to Posada, another estimable Mexican caricaturist, illustrator, and painter caught my attention and enlivened the visual landscape. Miguel Covarrubias (1904–1956) not only defined his time but arguably his work was influential beyond the border. He received more popularity in the United States than in Mexico, exerting influence on popular art through a refined yet original drawing style that helped define cosmopolitan, art moderne aesthetics of the late twenties and thirties through his contributions to the era's principal magazines, *Vanity Fair*, the *New Yorker*, and *Fortune*, among the most visible that published his work.

Many Mexican artists and designers worked in the United States and Europe, cross-pollinating their culture with the dominant international styles of the times. Look at some of the magazine layouts and typographic treatments for various artifacts herein and you will see how ancient Mexican forms had become contemporary. Mayan and Aztec design conceits, for instance, were seamlessly integrated into art deco motifs. At the same time, Russian constructivist and other European and American avant-gardes pervaded the Mexican visual language.

On my first and only pilgrimage to Mexico, made in the early eighties to witness the burgeoning Mexican protest movement, I toured the hot spots of Mexican popular and polemical art. I was blown away by the use of primary and secondary colors in the ultra-modernist home and studio of Diego Rivera, to the grand hacienda of Frida Kahlo, even to the walled fortress of Leon Trotsky. Mexico City was filled with surreal and socially symbolic art in abundance. Coming by chance across a richly endowed exhibition of Covarrubias drawings at a museum near Chapultepec Park was the pièce de résistance of my trip. Then in Oaxaca, my joy from seeing all the Day of the Dead souvenirs (thousands of miniature skeletons that filled the streets with color and comedy) and complemented by contemporary protest posters calling for equal rights and justice was evidence that design still played a huge role in Mexican culture.

This book contains all the artifacts that I was unable to locate on my expedition. The contents further prove Mexico to be a capital of graphic design exuberance—and an invaluable addition to the sociology of graphic endeavor.

# A WOOD TYPE MUSEUM GOES ANALOG

The 80,000-square-foot Hamilton Wood Type and Printing History Museum with its inventory of 1.5 million pieces of type, 300 vintage wood type fonts, and 6,000 wooden printing plates for posters and flyers is not yet digitized. But even if it was, so that all these artifacts were at everyone's fingertips, where's the fun in that?

Virtual reality is not touch-and-feel-roll-off-the-press reality. Digitalization cannot supplant what Hamilton's staff and volunteers do when they proudly guide visitors through the various hands-on experiences involving sixty-two printing presses and scores of other examples of printing apparatus from the original J. E. Hamilton Holly Wood Type Company in Two Rivers, Wisconsin. The tactile pleasures of handling type, ink, and paper to make printed pages dates back to the fifteenth century, when Johannes Gutenberg introduced movable type and altered the Western world. Today it is both inspirational and addictive (and not just from the fumes of linseed oil, either).

It is sobering to realize how much heavy lifting and physical exertion our ancestors went through to print everything from business cards to political manifestos—the original mass media. Type fonts were originally quite heavy, made from wood and metal. Of the two, wood was the more durable, produced in almost unlimited sizes and shapes. Metal was less scalable, although perfect for text and certain sized headlines. Wood was primarily used for large headlines on broadsides, posters, and placards and designed in bold, extra-bold, and ultra-bold weights in gothic and block-serif styles for eye-catching display. More elaborately engraved ornamental and dimensional faces were used for extravagances, like circus and carnival banners. These were artful but not pure art.

Wood type defined late nineteenth- and early twentieth-century America, when commerce was on the rise, railroads enabled interstate trade, and the advertising industry developed to "brand" and hawk consumables. Wood type is a historical treasure. Nonetheless, it does not get enough credit as the glue that bound both the image and message of the American experience together or that printing with it was the tool that made mass communications possible.

Founded by J. Edward Hamilton in 1880, the foundry was one of the largest manufacturers of wood typefaces (and drafting equipment) in the United States during the late nineteenth and twentieth centuries. The Hamilton museum exists today to promote wood type's relevance at a time when digital cloud is data storage heaven and archives are being compressed into bytes, like genies being sucked into their bottles. Among designers (and amateurs too), using vintage faces is now more popular than ever and learning their heritage is essential. So hands-on printing museums are gaining stature all over the world. Among them, Tipoteca Italiana, The Gutenberg Museum, and Plantin Moretus provide a direct link to the larger history of European culture and politics and in the United States the International Printing Museum, Andover Museum of Printing, the Printing Museum of Houston, and a host of other smaller venues curate tantalizing collections of printed matter and equipment. "We all have a story to tell and it's the story of visual communication and its place in history," says Bill Moran, the Hamilton's artistic director. Along with brother Jim Moran, the museum's director, their mission is to establish the relevancy of analog technology in a digital age, without resorting to nostalgia.

The Hamilton's annual Wayzgoose conference, which launched in 2009 in Two Rivers, about two hours north of Milwaukee, is a type mavens' and printers' tribal celebration. Wayzgoose refers to a common annual outing for the staffs of printing companies; printing associations also hold them so that participants can share their work as keepsakes and printing samples. Hamilton's is an exuberant mash-up of typeface and graphic designers, printers, and history buffs. It attracts a few hundred true believers—type pilgrims coming to Mecca—from all over the United States and beyond to share new techniques and discoveries. While there is lots of vintage stuff on hand, nostalgia is eschewed.

Jim and Bill Moran have been dedicated to growing the museum since it was contained in the original massive Hamilton Foundry complex (which was entirely demolished in 2013 to attract real estate development). Jim worked as a printer for his father Bernie Moran's Green Bay printing company and ran his own company; Bill is a printer and designer with his own letterpress storefront business in Minneapolis, Minnesota. The museum began in 1999 and they began volunteering in 2002 and were hired in 2009 to "help the museum tell its story," maintain equipment, create products for sale, publish a book, and improve the displays. "It's been a pleasant mayhem ever since," says Jim.

The Two Rivers Historical Society owns and operates the museum for the purpose of maintaining a working museum for hobbyists and experimental printers. But the Morans, along with assistant director Stephanie Carpenter, are pushing the museum to be more interactive for more visitors. The Wayzgoose conference and a slew of regularly scheduled workshops have helped attract a steady influx of visitors "who want to geek out on all things wood type." Of course, for those who cannot visit, the Hamilton has not forsaken the digital world: There is an online store and a partnership with the digital type foundry P22, which specializes in historical typeface revivals, and thus enabled them to develop a digital foundry. Last year Hamilton also launched an iPad app that tests font recognition skills. A partnership with Target in 2012 led to a line of clothing called Vintage Varsity. And they have commissioned designers to create brand-new wood typefaces. "All of this has gone a long way," Bill says, "to building awareness and sharing the museum's treasure trove of wood type and vintage printing plates," referring to their huge collections, such as around six trailer trucks full of antique theatrical poster art, wood blocks, and types from the Enquirer printing company.

This all contributes to what the Morans say is "preserving a way of communicating that still speaks to a new audience and needs to be saved and reconsidered for the high quality of its art." The practitioners who originally used these tools produces an incredibly brilliant form of illustrating, but "One can't simply separate old methods of printing from new ones based on a year or the technology."

# OSWALD COOPER'S BLACK BLITZ

Cooper Black is a truly twentieth-century type, as emblematic as Futura or Univers, but for very different reasons. While it was not the first face to have rounded serifs, it is the most demonstrative of the so-called fat faces. Used for advertising and editorial display, Cooper Black is as eye-catching as a charging bull and as loud as a carnival barker.

Oswald Cooper (1879–1940), Oz or Ozzie to his associates, was the man behind the face. Cooper was a native of Coffeyville, Kansas. In his teens he settled in Chicago to pursue an illustration career. He eventually became one of the progenitors of the so-called Chicago style. In the early 1920s and 1930s American design was a mélange of regional dialects, each emanating from a big city under the influence of a single person's mannerism or the confluence of a few. Lettering, typography, and illustration were the primary mass media. Advertising was the main outlet. The Boston style was attributable to W. A. Dwiggins and the New York style to Frederic W. Goudy (both spent time in Chicago), but Cooper founded the Chicago (also known as the Midwest) style. He combined calligraphic skill with typographic expertise to create advertisements that were modern in character and classic in form. While respecting tradition, he understood the needs of an expanding mass commercial market.

Cooper stumbled into his lifelong vocation by accident. He left the comforts of his Kansas home at eighteen, bound for Chicago to study at the Frank Holme School of Illustration. There, he was inspired by his lettering teacher, Frederic W. Goudy, to pursue a broader practice. Goudy, the most prolific of all American type designers and director of Holme's typographic department, befriended Oz and helped him earn his tuition by assigning him jobs setting type for correspondence school booklets.

While teaching at Holme, Cooper met Fred Bertsch, who ran an art-service agency next door to the school. Bertsch admired Cooper's craft and in 1904 they entered into the perfect partnership; Bertsch, a consummate salesman, and Cooper, the gifted artist, formed Bertsch & Cooper, a full-service type shop, including typesetting layout, copywriting, and design. As a small studio Bertsch & Cooper based its initial reputation on hand lettering for small local jobs and later large national campaigns. Eventually, their financial success allowed Cooper the opportunity to test his other talents. "Cooper, of course, had brilliant capacities as a craftsman in the field of printing and of advertising layout," wrote typographer Paul Standard in *The Book of Oz Cooper*

(The Society of Typographic Arts, Chicago, 1949). "But in his endowment was also a gift for language, and through its discipline a power of clear and forthright expression. . . . His text sought to persuade, not stampede."

The quality of Cooper's lettering was equal to the strength of his writing. Cooper's letterforms were not simply novelties, but "lessons in structural form, in free and friendly balance," wrote Standard. Cooper created as many new designs as he could. Yet he had an instinctual distrust of things superficially modish and conceptually strained. "Types too dexterous, like tunes too luscious," he once waxed, "are predestinated (sic) to short careers."

Actually, Cooper stumbled into type design almost as accidentally as he did lettering. His first type was drawn from a cut, unbeknownst to Cooper and without his permission, in 1913 by one of Morris Fuller Benton's staff artists at American Type Foundry (ATF). Cooper had routinely created customized lettering in advertisements for one of Bertsch & Cooper's largest clients, the Packard Motor Car Company. The ads were so widely seen that the lettering caught Benton's eye. Type pirating was a fact of life, and ads were neither signed nor attributed to any artist. Benton immediately ordered the type redrawn and founded in metal, and called it Packard.

Shortly afterward, Barnhart Brothers & Spindler Type Foundry (BB&S), America's second largest, approached Cooper to design a complete family based on his lettering. Cooper did not immediately accept the offer, reasoning that he was first a lettering artist, not a type designer. Bertsch called Cooper the "Michelangelo of lettering," and urged him to accept BB&S's offer. In 1918 Cooper's first typeface was released, named Cooper, and later renamed Cooper Old Style.

In the early 1900s typefaces were vigorously marketed to printers and type shops, often through ambitious type specimen sheets designed with the same artistic flourish as period sheet music. BB&S was particularly aggressive and succeeded in popularizing Cooper's first normal-weight roman (Cooper). They further made it the basis for a continuing family. The second in the series was Cooper Black, the most novel of early-twentieth-century super-bolds. BB&S declared that Cooper Black as "the selling type supreme, the multibillionaire sales type, it made big advertisements out of little ones." Cooper responded that his invention was "for far-sighted printers with near-sighted customers." Owing to its novelty, it caused commotion in certain conservative circles. "The slug-machine makers thundered against the black 'menace.' But the trend was on—the advertising world accepted the black in a thoroughgoing way and the orders rolled up in a volume never before known for any type face," wrote a type seller of the day.

Other related type designs followed in quick succession in what became known as "the black blitz."

Cooper Italic was described by Cooper as "much closer to its parent pen form than the roman." Cooper Hilite was made by the simple expedient of painting a white highlight on a black proof of Cooper Black, with patterns cut and matrices engraved accordingly. "It's good for sparkling headlines; it cannot be crowded like the black, but must have plenty of 'air,'" wrote Cooper. Cooper Black Italic was completed in 1926 to cash in on the surge in sales of Cooper Black. Cooper Black Condensed was designed shortly afterward to have 20 percent less heft and be generally more useful. A complete metal font of Cooper Black weighed almost eighty-three pounds and strained the back of many a typesetter, so the condensed version was thought to save on costly chiropractor bills.

Cooper initiated trends, but he refused to take part in "the itch of the times." Nor was he a fan of what in 1928 he called "the balmy wing of modernism." However, his last face, designed in 1929 for BB&S, originally called Cooper Fullface and later changed in ATF catalogs to Cooper Modern, was, in fact, consistent with the dominant styles. Of this face Cooper wrote, "This style, lately revived by the practitioners of the 'modernistic' typography, has created a demand for display letters that comport well with it—letters that reflect the sparkling contrasts of Bodoni, and that carry weight to meet the needs of advertisers. Cooper Fullface is such a letter."

Before his death in 1940 Cooper turned his attention to the fight for copyright protections for himself and all designers. He tried to convince the government that patents should be awarded for typefaces. He also chided his colleagues about copying: "To work in the style of current trends or past periods is all right, but do it in your own way. Study the work of the leaders, but never have another's work before you when you are trying to create. There was never a great imitator—not even in vaudeville. The way to become a master is by cultivating your own talent."

# PART 5:
# CONVERSATIONS

# MOTHER
# OF ROBOTS

---

## INTERVIEW WITH CARLA DIANA

---

The term robotic implies a machine as simulacrum of a human that walks and talks haltingly and serves its master. Remember Woody Allen playing the robot butler in the film *Sleeper* or the *Star Wars* smart-aleck C-3PO. It is tempting to stereotype robots as humorous machines. In science fiction as in real life, robot designers and engineers have imbued machines with characteristics/personalities that make them more "friendly," albeit sometimes exasperating. Yet the definition of a robot goes beyond the humanoid model. Carla Diana, a product designer and technologist who chairs the 4D Design Department at Cranbrook, discusses the increasingly more nuanced ways of introducing robots into everyday life in her new book *My Robot Gets Me: How Social Design Can Make New Products More Human*. She examines how the current generation of smart products are not as smart as we think. She includes many mundane machines and automatic devices in the robot genre, and this she says is only the beginning, the early stages. More conceptualizing is yet to come. Her delightful and insightful book focuses on innovative design as a means to better integrate robotics into daily life, even beyond already incredible features, like a Tesla automobile that is programmed (or trained, if you prefer) to pick you up on its own. You might say that Diana advocates, indeed is the mother of, housebroken machines. She is an elegant thinker whose ideas will change our perception of the smart machines in our midst and to come.

**Steven Heller: It takes awhile to get used to some of the terminology in our new world. Like "friend" is not friendship, "smart" does not signify bright, "social" implies a network of users. Computers have changed the vocabulary but must they also alter behavior?**

**Carla Diana:** Right! There is a lot of terminology that is specific to the area of our newly connected, sometimes robot-driven products. I do think that computers change our human behavior in many ways. We often don't even realize that it's taking place. Just as you've mentioned, terms that have a certain connotation in our human world having a different meaning for products, and the reverse is true. We might talk about needing a "recharge" if we are tired, and needing to "calibrate" thoughts to be on the same page with another person.

Treating machines as part of the family is a big expectation! There isn't necessarily room in a household for new family members, both from a physical and a psychic point of view, but we can certainly grow to love and depend on certain products. I think they are family members in the way that pets are family members, that is, we depend on a dog's presence for comfort, distraction, slipper delivery, etc., but the relationship isn't necessarily front and center in terms of all the social interactions taking place in a room at a given time.

**SH: What is social design and how are you and others integrating social design into products?**

**CD:** Social design, as I discuss it in *My Robot Gets Me*, is an overarching strategy for creative direction that places the dynamics of a relationship between a person and a product at the center of all design activities. Rather than thinking about the form, interaction, materials and any other aspects as separate, siloed activities, it asks for a holistic approach that looks at all of those characteristics through a social lens. The book lays out a framework to aid in keeping these myriad aspects in mind, starting with the physical presence, moving on to the way an object expresses itself through light, sound and movement, then a look at how it interacts in diverse contexts and ultimately how it exists within an ecosystem of other products in a person's life.

My colleagues in the design world and I are using this approach to conceive of new products, such as the hospital robot, Moxi, that is developed by Diligent Robotics, for which I serve as head of design. I have used social design techniques such as scenario storyboarding and bodystorming, or "acting out" a range of interactions in order to work with the team to conceive of the robot's behavior in diverse situations. This type of planning helps the team maintain a unified ideal for what the robot should be and do, providing core guidance for design decisions and also helping people in different disciplines (engineering, software development, marketing, etc.) to understand why the design details are the way they are.

**SH: You cite statistics on how many "elderly" people have adopted smart products. Would you say that the learning curves are now short enough to accommodate their resistance or have we, who grew up with this stuff, just gotten older, more experienced, and wiser?**

**CD:** I think it's a combination of those two phenomena coming together. As time goes on, we will have more adults who grew up as "digital natives," like my son, who knew how to navigate a mobile device interface from the time he was one year old (if not earlier), and as these adults get older, they are more accustomed to common interaction patterns and frequently used design affordances. At the same time, social design emerges from designers' ability to create intuitive interfaces due to the affordability and accessibility of more sophisticated components and development. The two experiences go hand in hand.

**SH: You run the 4D Design department at Cranbrook. What is 4D?**

**CD:** The 4D Design program at Cranbrook offers a two-year MFA program and is focused on exploring critical questions about the world around us through creative applications of emerging technology. It's based on the practice of tangible interaction, that is, the design of artifacts that harness both the physical and the digital. It includes everything from augmented reality to applied robotics and 3D printing, and the essence of it is around products and experiences that are responsive. The common thread is that all of these things will have the ability to change over time through intrinsic behaviors such as light patterns, sound, motion and other dynamic displays. (The fourth "D" is time!)

4D Design offers the opportunity to build a hybrid design practice where the creative and the technical hold equal weight. It encourages a holistic look at dynamic design elements as well as a focus on overall context in terms of place, time and ergonomics. Rather than having designers relegated to thinking only about what's on a screen, we are finally at a place and time where the value of thinking about how spaces and objects can be imbued with data and interact with people is more clearly recognized.

**SH: How do you see 4D as integrating into our future lives?**

**CD:** I see 4D integrating into our lives in the near future through an increasing number of everyday objects that have programmed, embedded electronics, and therefore the ability to take advantage of the dynamic behaviors that I talk about in the book and in my teaching at Cranbrook, that is, the ability to understand people's intentions through sophisticated inputs like touch, voice, and gesture and then respond with expressive behaviors based on light, sound, and movement. This may mean a chandelier that can adjust its position, color, and brightness to be appropriate to the context of a social gathering or a bin that can navigate office hallways and facilitate recycling.

**SH: You devote a chapter to the complexities of communication between product and person. Does this require an evolutionary adaptation?**

**CD:** I hope not! The benefit of social design is to piggyback on the behaviors that we've already developed and that are ingrained in us through just moving around the world and doing what humans know how to do. Rather than requiring an evolutionary adaptation, I see people and their products adapting to one another to take advantage of a kind of "shorthand" communication, where a product may understand an abbreviated, spoken turn of phrase ("Alexa, timer, 3 minutes"), and a person can understand the modalities that the product can display, like a pulsing light or short tone to indicate that your coffee is ready.

**SH: Robots are envisioned in many forms and called by different names. Do you foresee a standardized definition of robot?**

**CD:** The definition of "robot" is an interesting, esoteric question that my students and I in the 4D program at Cranbrook grapple with on a regular basis. It's common to think of robots as those mythical creature-like machines from science fiction, whereas in my book I challenge the reader to think of things like microphones and desk lamps as robots. Rather than foreseeing a standardized definition, I think that robotics applied to everyday objects, when done well, will become so commonplace that we won't think of them as robots anymore, they will just be enhanced versions of whatever the traditional object might be, like an automated ottoman or a responsive task lamp. The idea of "robot" will cease to feel foreign or separate from an object that has a more established identity.

**SH: And, if so, will there be a set of social mores that will apply to smart machines? Will we one day see a robot bill of rights?**

**CD:** I do think there will be social mores that apply to smart machines. There are interesting studies that show that we respond with compassion to objects if we perceive of them as being the slightest bit autonomous. The MIT researcher Kate Darling has several research papers based on workshops where people object to torturing "baby dinosaur" Pleo robots and hesitate to smash hammers onto crude buglike robots. Rather than a bill of rights, I think it will be more like loose social expectations and behaviors of etiquette that emerge from culture, you know, like the way one pours tea or which fork to use. It may be considered déclassé to kick the delivery robot. Oh, and by the way, when I'm home with my five-year-old I insist on using courtesies with our conversational agents; I say, "Alexa, stop please" or "Siri, set a timer for 10 minutes please." It's less about the robot having feelings than just a general modeling of expectations around how we treat one another in social situations.

**SH: Smart machines exist to serve mankind, but how far does this service go when you name and design machines with human traits?**

**CD:** This is a tricky one that's been coming up a lot! It's one that I think about when it comes to race and gender because many of the robots that I design have connotations based on their color, materials, and the way that the form leans toward one gender or another. For example, with hospital service robots it's helpful to design them to feel like "part of the team." In a largely female workforce that may mean leaning toward female characteristics, but then there is the risk of reinforcing a gender stereotype simply through the robot's presence, which isn't great in the long run.

And as far as service goes, well, I won't go down the X-rated path today, but let's just say that with any emerging technology the porn industry tends to innovate more quickly than any other in the commercial realm.

# FRESH ARAB TYPE HISTORY

## INTERVIEW WITH BAHIA SHEHAB & HAYTHAM NAWAR

**Y**our book *A History of Arab Graphic Design* appears to be modeled to an extent on Philip B. Meggs's *A History of Graphic Design*, even down to the "A" in the title. Do you believe that this is just peeling off the first layer of Arab design?

Of course, Meggs's history is an influential reference, the fact that most history books on the topic are quite Western-centric in their discourse was reason enough for us to feel that the narrative has to shift. The "A" was added by our editor Nadia Naqib, who agrees with us on the fact that *A History of Arab Graphic Design* is the first book on the topic and it is only our take on it, and we hope to read future works by scholar colleagues who will hopefully reflect on our book and build on it. As we like to mention, the content of the book represents only one-third of the material we have. When the book was published, more people showed interest in contributing to our second edition of the book. We are receiving even more content from countries that we did not cover extensively in this edition (e.g., Algeria, Sudan, Yemen, UAE).

**SH: How long have you been working on this book, and where has your support come from?**

**BS & HN:** The idea for the book came about ten years ago when the course with the same title was developed for the graphic design program at the American University in Cairo by Bahia, but we had no textbook to teach it. It took our research team and us over two years of hard work to collect the data. Then, another year for cowriting, which was more than we initially expected because of the amount and diversity of content that we had gathered. This book is only the starting point, and, in a future edition, we hope to include more material. The American University in Cairo supported the project financially in the form of a research grant, in addition to the great resources that are available at our Rare Books and Special Collections Library. Many designers, artists, and collectors were very generous in donating their work and providing information and oral histories. The families of deceased artists and designers also provided some of the work and narratives. We tried to reach people via emails and commissioned students and young professionals to help us collect data, visit archives, and conduct interviews. A lot of people contributed to making this book possible, and we are very grateful to the enthusiasm and hard work that was put along the process.

**SH: Arab calligraphy has been covered in other volumes. What, if anything, new did you discover about this history?**

**BS & HN:** In this volume, we explored the contribution of Arab calligraphers to the field of graphic design, especially in modern times. We look at calligraphy as part of the vernacular culture. The examples we show to focus on print media, shop signs, street signs, and other applications. The main new idea presented in the book is the continuity of a design visual language from Islamic cultural history to modern and contemporary design applications. Calligraphy was an integral visual element in a glorious past, it was interesting to trace the devolution of the script through mediums. Its humble transformation into typeset molds, then its journey into the typewriter and later transfer sheets, and finally into the digital world. It was like witnessing the rise and fall of nations across decades simply by the shape of their script.

**SH: What triggered the beginning of modern Arab graphic design?**

**BS & HN:** The late nineteenth century and the beginning of the twentieth century witnessed the foundation of art education in the Arab world. This was one of the factors for the development of generations of Arab artists and designers. Education in the field played a major role in allowing professions in art and design to flourish. In the same period, several magazines and newspapers were formed, opening opportunities for these graduates to be hired in publishing houses and practice what they have learned. The demand for designers in different aspects resulted in calligraphers, art directors, cover designers, and other "design"-related crafts to surface. It was a flourishing time in the history of Arab periodicals, and it coincided with the emergence of educated talents. On top of this, the Egyptian cinema and theater industry was also flourishing and demanding artists and designers from the region. Similarly, the publishing field was prospering in Lebanon.

**SH: I won't go chapter by chapter, but each era does have defining characteristics. Did Arab graphic design develop in parallel or separately from Western design?**

**BS & HN:** The relation between Arab graphic design and Western graphic design is complicated. In the book, we tried to show the link between the work of designers and the sociopolitical events that were unfolding at their time in addition to the geopolitical situation. This being said, history witnessed a long tradition of colonialism in the region, which justifies the complicated Arab-Western relation. From a pedagogical perspective, the design is tied to the community and its different problems. Hence, you cannot separate design from society, politics, economy, and culture.

**SH: The Arab world is rather large and diverse. You work and live in Egypt. Was there a preponderance of design produced in any single country or was it all about equal?**

**BS & HN:** Out of the almost eighty designers documented in the book, forty are from Egypt. This speaks to the scale and weight of Egypt as a regional knowledge generation center. Lebanon, Syria, and Iraq all had thriving intellectual, social, and political realities. Finding material was not equal in every country. Obviously, because we are Cairo based and because, historically, Egypt has been a cultural center with several creative industries thriving, a lot of the material is from Egypt. Work from countries like Palestine, Lebanon, Iraq, and Syria is also well represented but some countries were very difficult to access. We have low representation from countries like Libya, Algeria, and Yemen due to the difficulty of travel to these countries. We also have no representation from the Arabian Gulf, keeping in mind that we chose to stop documenting in the early 2000s; it is definitely a different landscape now. The North African countries that were colonized by the French had design work that did not contain the Arabic language, thus we had to eliminate it for now. It was a difficult decision not to include designs by Arab designers who utilize the Latin script only in their work but we thought it best and simply as a selection tool.

**SH: What are the main influences on the work you address? Are there national distinctions or design vocabularies that are obvious to your eyes but not the untrained eye?**

**BS & HN:** When it comes to influences, there is a predominance of the Islamic visual language that can be seen reappearing and reemerging with time. Several artists like Helmi El Touni and Mohieddine el-Labbad were inspired by Islamic art, the art of the book, and the complexity of the relationship between Arabic script and images. In addition to Islamic influence, there are visual elements specific to each civilization. For example, in Egypt, some designers borrow elements from Ancient Egyptian visual language, and in Syria and Iraq, they were inspired by Sumerian and cuneiform. It is interesting to see the different historical references integrated into today's visual language. Also, some designers use vernacular art as a reference in Egypt and Palestine or African art in the Maghreb.

**SH: Over the past twenty years, there has been considerable interest in and development of Arabic type and typography. What accounts for this surge of interest?**

**BS & HN:** Generally speaking, in the last twenty years, there has been interest in Arab type and typography but also in Arab design at large. This is due to a generation searching for a new visual identity that represents their culture in a globalized world. Language and the way language looks is a reflection of identity. In the early nineties and after the Lebanese war, new design programs developed in Lebanon, and others in the region followed. This gave rise to young designers who were now exposed to and forced to become part of a global design culture. They had to find answers for new Arab visual representation and they are still developing solutions. Design is in our every day and is at the forefront of this representation of local history and cultural heritage. We think that creative producers are the real cultural ambassadors of nations.

**SH: In Meggs's book, he divides his chronology into stylistic manifestations. Do you see similar distinctions or any period styles emerge?**

**BS & HN:** We are still working on finding these patterns. We think that as we collect more data we will be able to trace more stylistic developments. But there were definitely waves linked to political and social events that led to an increase in creative production across the Arab world. During the 1920s till the '50s and even '60s for some countries, as Arab nations were decolonizing on the ground, artists and designers were looking for a new visual language that represents them and that is different from that of the colonizer. So there was a wave of historical visual references during that period whether ancient Egyptian, Phoenician, Sumerian, or others. During the 1960s and the 1970s as governments of nations like Egypt, Syria and Iraq started sending their artists to study at universities in Russia and Europe; they also came back with visual influences that were clear in their work. Some artists went to China during this time, and this had a lifelong influence on their work. We are still scratching the surface here so we are hoping to find more threads as more data comes in.

**SH: Is there an Arabic modern, postmodern, new wave?**

**BS & HN:** This is a trick question as it references art and design from the Arab world again through a Western lens. The debate is ongoing but we can safely say that as the world was developing ideas on modernism, postmodernism, and other major movements, there were definitely Arab artists and designers who were reflecting on these same ideas in their work. In addition to that there were local concerns that were beyond and different to what was being developed in the United States and Europe. As mentioned earlier, a search for an individual identity linked to heritage, whether ancient, Islamic, Coptic, and many others, was evident. There was also a look at forgotten local and vernacular languages and a revival of that. So the question is not whether there was, but what else?

**SH: What would you say you learned as researchers that is your most profound discovery?**

**BS & HN:** The continuity of ideas about human dignity, independence, and identity in spite of dislocation, colonization, invasion, and social upheavals was very fascinating to witness. It was beautiful to see how emotional designers would get when talking or sharing their work with us, and in some cases even when they refused to do so. Some of the most productive and experimental designers were also cultural activists and concerned citizens who cared deeply about their nations. We also discovered that the idea of graphic design is yet to be well understood in the region. Due to the lack of institutional and governmental attention and support, some designers viewed their design work as a commercial practice, not as important as art for example. In addition to this, because of colonial history and oppressive regimes, some designers were afraid to show and/or publish their work due to past sociopolitical tensions around certain topics, and they did not want their name to be linked to certain events. The discoveries were so many, the artwork, the human stories of these designers, their relationship to each other and their reactions to political and social events unfolding during their time. One of the things that we are still looking for is the history of female designers of the region.

**SH: What do you want the readers to take away from your book? How should it be used in the Arab world and in the West too?**

**BS & HN:** We hope that the book will become a cornerstone for the canon in the region. It is mainly targeting students of art and design, emerging designers and artists, art and design historians, and anyone interested in the history of visual culture in the Arab world. Concerning the Arab world, we would like for this book to fill a generation gap. It should serve as an educational tool for our students and for the coming generations to learn about the richness of their heritage and history. We would also like to shift the narrative on the global history of graphic design and we hope to inspire scholars from different regions to also contribute to this global history that has been Western and Eurocentric for a long time. In general, we would like for the general public—the people who are not artists or designers by education—to realize the importance of design and acknowledge the link with cultural heritage.

# STUCK ON THE SWISS GRID

## INTERVIEW WITH ALLON SCHOENER

In 1957, Allon Schoener (b.1926), a cultural historian and museum curator, among other achievements, at the forefront of important design exhibitions, curated the first "Swiss Graphic Designers" exhibition in the United States at The Cincinnati Contemporary Arts Center. It was circulated by the AIGA to New York, Boston, Manchester, La Jolla, Milwaukee, Akron, Milwaukee, and Chicago, among other venues. It originated after Schoener had met Armin Hofmann at Aspen the previous year. The exhibition catalog was designed with a preface by Noel Martin. (www.nytimes .com/2009/02/28/arts/design/28martin.html). The exhibition included the exemplars of the Basel and Zurich practices, Adolf Flückiger, Karl Gerstner, Armin Hofmann, Gottfried Honegger, Richard P. Lohse, Nelly Rudin, Max Schmid, Carlo Vivarelli, Emil Ruder, Hans Neuberg, Siegfried Odermatt, and Josef Müller-Brockmann. "The exhibition procures an insight into the working habits of several Swiss commercial artists who distinguish themselves through their objectivity and austerity of the creative media," Müller-Brockmann wrote in his Introduction.

Objectivity and order are hallmarks of the Swiss Style. Or as Martin wrote: "The term geometric has been applied to Swiss graphic design. It may be a useful label but its connotation tends to limit its scope. With a definite point of view there is a wide range of solutions possible. A number of American designers show an affinity to this point of view. Whether the influences are direct or not, does matter. I must confess I think they are." As the first exhibition to expose this work in America, "We hope that this exhibition as it travels . . . will reveal to designers and their clients what can be accomplished by an open-minded attitude and a desire to present the facts honestly, without gimmicks, unfunny humor, redundancy and coupons." Martin wrote that the exhibition may have resulted from his "personal enthusiasm" but it was Schoener as curator and Dorli Hofmann (Dorothea Hofmann) as expediter of the material from Switzerland, who made it happen. I recently asked Schoener to tell us more about what led up to this landmark design exhibition in the United States.

**Steven Heller: I believe 1957 was within the period when Swiss graphic design was more or less at its high-water mark in terms of world acceptance and certainly American adaptation. What forces formed this event?**

**Allon Schoener:** I don't agree with "1957 was within the period when Swiss graphic design was more or less at its highwater mark in terms of world acceptance and certainly American adaptation." Perhaps it was known in other countries, but I believe that it was not accepted in the United States until the 1960s and that this exhibition accelerated its acceptance. *Print* and *Interiors* of that period are available online and would confirm my position. Dorli Hofmann would also confirm it. From 1958 to 1965 saw the publication of the seminal Swiss design magazine *Neue Grafik*, edited by Zürich-based graphic designers Richard Paul Lohse (1902–1988), Josef Müller-Brockmann (1914–1996), Hans Neuburg (1904–1983), and Carlo Vivarelli (1919–1986). The entire set of magazines was reprinted in 2015 by Lars Muller Verlag.

From 1950 to 1955, I was a curator at the San Francisco Museum of Art and worked with many graphic designers. There were no expressions of interest in Swiss graphic design. At that time, I was an acolyte of Charles and Ray Eames. Although Swiss graphic design was hardly their thing, they were into the latest design discoveries and would have mentioned it.

**SH: I bow to you on this for certain. Can you further discuss the origin of this exhibition and what triggered your interest?**

**AS:** [It was] through Noel Martin. I had done an exhibition of Will Burtin's work at the Cincinnati Contemporary Arts Center [where Martin was design director]. Will was on the planning committee and invited me to go to the Aspen International Design Conference in 1956. I went and subsequently became a member of the conference planning committee.

For the 1956 conference, Armin Hofmann and Josef Muller-Brockmann had been invited as guests. At that time, the spirit of the Aspen Design Conference was discovery. Armin and Muller-Brockmann presented their work and the work of their colleagues. Although I was hardly a specialist in graphic design, it was apparent to me that there would be an audience for a traveling exhibition and began discussions with Armin and Muller-Brockmann. Dorli Hofmann [Armin Hofmann's wife] was a participant and served as coordinator because she was fluent in English.

**SH: How was the content of this exhibition put together?**

**AS:** They, as a group, decided whose work would be exhibited and proceeded to collect and send exhibition materials. I accepted their selections and planned the design accordingly. I also organized the itinerary.

**SH: What was the response to the exhibition?**

**AS:** I don't recall any publicity. It was at the AIGA in New York and nothing special happened. As you can see from the itinerary, it was seen in other cities.

**SH: What were you hoping to accomplish with the exhibition that was new and enlightening?**

**AS:** As I mentioned above, I was an acolyte of Charles and Ray Eames. I was influenced by their thirst for discovery. To me, Swiss graphic design was a discovery—hardly known or appreciated. If it had been a hot topic in this country, Connie [Mildred Constantine, who was curator of many MoMA design exhibitions, would have done an exhibition at MoMA]. My exhibition obviated that need. She had done an exhibition of Herbert Bayer.

**SH: Would you agree or disagree that there was tension between the Swiss moderns and a more eclectic approach to type and design?**

**AS:** Agree absolutely. To the best of my knowledge, there were no art schools where they taught graphic design. People studied painting, sculpture, and illustration. Their graphic designs were influenced by all three. Raymond Lowey's extravagant sense of design had an impact on graphic design.

**SH: The exhibition introduced those who are now called the pioneers of Swiss design. How did you frame their work for an American audience?**

**AS:** Being in the museum business at that time, discovery and exhibition were cardinal principles. So, I saw Swiss Graphic Design as a discovery for art audiences in general and graphic designers in particular.

**SH: Did you embrace Swiss design as a revolutionary or evolutionary movement drawing inspiration from the Bauhaus?**

**AS:** Unquestionably, there is a Bauhaus heritage; however, I did not see a need to get into that. In fact, a curator could not possibly illustrate the roots of every exhibition. This was an exhibition of a contemporary phenomenon.

**SH: Your exhibition is evidence of an historical moment. Would you say that it had an impact on design education in America?**

**AS:** Although I would like to think that the exhibition had a profound impact, I doubt that is true. I think that it reached an audience of cognoscenti; they in turn, might have carried the message to a wider audience. This could explain the eventual broad acceptance of Swiss graphic designers in this country.

# DAVID KING IS ABSOLUTELY RELENTLESS

- - - - - - - - - - - - - - - - - - - - - - - - - - -

## INTERVIEW WITH RICK POYNOR

- - - - - - - - - - - - - - - - - - - - - - - - - - -

**T**wenty-five years ago I started a brief correspondence with David King, the former UK art director of the London *Sunday Times Magazine*. The publication was one of the most exquisite Sunday supplements of the era and, for me, a delicacy. I was thrilled when he returned my letter agreeing to be interviewed for *PRINT* magazine. Regrettably, I dragged my feet for much too long, was then childishly too embarrassed to conduct the interview and he passed away in 2016. What an unforgivably missed opportunity. So, that's why I am grateful to critic and historian Rick Poynor for spending the past years working on his biographical monograph of King, *David King: Designer, Activist, Visual Historian* (Yale University Press). And, I'm doubly pleased that it is such an exceptional book in its informative text and well-edited images (smartly designed by Simon Esterson), worthy of its protagonist and extra valuable to graphic design and political graphics history.

King was a uniquely intelligent graphic designer. Not only did he reintroduce the language of Russian Constructivism to design through the form and content of his own books, he further provided the necessary social, cultural, and political context for the art and design of the Soviet period (and before). King was not a mere stylist but a practical historian. He did not just mine the past for usable conceits, he chronicled a tumultuous epoch of the 20th century from a socio-visual perspective that, in turn, opened our eyes to the ripple effect of politics on design and aesthetics (i.e., form and function).

Poynor has taken the opportunity to document King's life as a means to analyze how ideology impacts design and how design influences messaging in our increasingly branded world. I've long admired his work as founding editor of *Eye* magazine and author of critical essays and books that define Postmodern typographic history. This book takes the reader down another historical route and the David King website provides another dimension for deeper study and appreciation of King and his work as author, practitioner, curator and advocate. I asked Poynor to talk about why King's work and this book are so relevant for designers today.

**Steven Heller: Why did you decide to do a monograph on David King?**

**Rick Poynor:** I wanted to do a monograph on King for years. He was always one of the designers I admired most because of the breadth, complexity, and impact of his work as graphic designer, visual journalist, photographer, collector, and author of books. He was a fascinating and exciting person to be around. In 2016, I was about to ask him whether he'd agree to a book when he died unexpectedly. Later in the year, as a result of the initiative of Simon Esterson, designer and co-owner of *Eye* magazine, I met Judy Groves and Valerie Wade of King's estate to discuss the possibility of a book. Suddenly, with Judy and Valerie's backing, the project was possible, and it developed from there, with Simon and I as a team from the start.

**SH: His work has made a major contribution to American design without most Americans knowing his name. Why did King not have the same kind of visibility as other UK designers?**

**RP:** King's period of concentrating on being a graphic designer runs from 1963 to the end of the 1980s. In his day, he won a lot of design awards. He stepped back with the arrival of the computer. It just didn't interest him. He started authoring books while he was still art editor of the *Sunday Times Magazine* in London: *Trotsky: A Documentary* (1972) was the first. He built up a vast, world-class collection of graphics, publications, photographs, and artifacts from the Russian Revolution and Stalinist era. By the end of the 1980s, his photo library had become a business. So, in the computer era, he was off the radar for most designers, and he wasn't part of the debates about graphic authorship, even though he is in many ways an ultimate example of the phenomenon.

Meanwhile, through books such as *The Commissar Vanishes* (1997) and *Red Star Over Russia* (2009), his work achieved a public visibility that went way beyond the design scene. *Life* magazine featured him. His books received serious reviews in the *New York Times Book Review* and the *New York Review of Books*, and that press attention happened across Europe, too. My hope with the monograph and the website is to bring King's achievement back into view. He is one of Britain's finest designers.

**SH: He was among the first of the literal postmodernists to inject Russian Constructivism into his work. Was he consciously trying to revive the Soviet aesthetic?**

**RP:** No, he wasn't. He never called himself a postmodernist, and I'm sure he would have rejected the concept and the term. He was no kind of historicist. In the early to mid-1980s, some of his magazine work, covers for *City Limits* and page designs for *Crafts*, have a slightly "new wave" look to them. This had nothing to do with music or fashion. He arrived at these historical sources from a different direction, grounded in tenacious historical research for his collection. He was drawn to Constructivism because it was dynamic, direct, and forceful, and Russian revolutionary graphics made maximum use of limited means—two colors and poor printing. King faced the same technical limitations when designing low-cost political posters for anti-racist and anti-apartheid causes in the late 1970s and early 1980s. It was never about style for its own sake, though he was clearly a highly expressive manipulator of graphic form. In fact, he admired the political photomontages of John Heartfield most of all.

SH: I recall the first book I bought of King's was the Ali book, and it blew me away. Rodchenko was the second (in fact, my wife "redesigned" the jacket for the US audience). Then one by one I acquired his collection-based books. Where did this obsession with vintage graphics, manipulated photographs, and all the other tools of propaganda that he collected and catalogued come from?

RP: In 1970, while working on the *Sunday Times Magazine*, King visited Moscow for the first time to undertake visual research for a story about Vladimir Lenin to mark the centenary of the revolutionary politician's birth. He also inquired about pictures of Leon Trotsky, but Trotsky had been brushed out of history, and officials declined to help him. King returned to London with the first pieces in his Russian collection and an unquenchable desire to locate more. He was already a collector of items relating to movies, crime, politics, and space exploration for use in his visual journalism. His friend and collaborator Judy Groves suggested he concentrate on Russian history, which rapidly became his main concern.

He was absolutely relentless in his searches, traveling widely and mailing out want-lists to antiquarian bookshops and dealers across Europe and America. For instance, it took him years to put together a complete set of *USSR in Construction* magazines in all five languages, but they could still be found in dusty corners back then, if you knew where to look, for relatively small sums. Try doing that now! It's an extraordinary archive and it can be seen today at Tate Britain in London, which acquired the entire collection shortly before King died.

# BRAVE NEW BOOK DESIGN

- - - - - - - - - - - - - - - - -
## INTERVIEW WITH DON WALL
- - - - - - - - - - - - - - - - -

**A**rchitect Don Wall curated Italian-born Paolo Soleri's 1970 retrospective of his radical architecture at the Corcoran Gallery of Art in Washington, DC. Arcosanti, as originally designed by Soleri, was intended for five thousand people; it was located near Cordes Junction, about seventy miles north of Phoenix, Arizona, and was a magnet for many idealistic artist/designers who joined the building teams. The goal of the project was to provide a model that can demonstrate Soleri's concept of Arcology, a new combination of architecture in sync with ecology—a forerunner of today's environmental sustainability movement. Because the exhibit was going to travel to the Whitney and to Chicago, Berkeley, and other cities, Praeger Publishers knew there would be a guaranteed audience. When they asked if Wall, who never designed a book before, would do the book, he said "sure" and went to a local bookstore "to buy a $2 paperback on how to make a book." That volume, *Visionary Cities: the Arcology of Paolo Soleri* (1971), in the tradition of Quentin Fiore's books for Marshall McLuhan, became a radical departure for book design of the era and helped define Soleri as an influential experimental architect. I've admired and studied the book for ages. This was the first time I had an opportunity to discuss the design with Wall.

**Steven Heller: You are an architect not a book designer, so how did you come to design a book on Paolo Soleri and what inspired the manner in which you designed it?**

**Don Wall:** My architectural training in the 1950s at University of Manitoba involved solving design problems, anything from an embassy in India, to a chair, to uniforms. I treated the book as a manipulable thing, not unlike a cup. The origin of my approach to the book was due, in part, to the first lecture I heard by Prof. Jim Donohue. He talked about how the front elevation of Rietveld's Schröder House remained compositionally balanced when rotated in space. Rietveld introduced the idea of nongravitational architecture by removing architecture from the ground plane. Likewise I wanted to remove the book from the belly as ground plane for it being read. Consequently, there's no single directionality. To read it you have to rotate the book vertically, horizontally, not just once or twice, but continually. At one point the pages fold out to six feet long, increasing its three-dimensionality as an object existing in space.

**SH: How much input was there from Soleri himself?**

DW: None.

**SH: I know he was a cultlike figure with followers coming to the desert to work with him on his projects. Were you one of those followers?**

DW: I was not a follower, nor an apprentice. My first contact with Soleri was in 1968 when I spent a week and a half with him and his family at their Cosanti residence in Arizona. Walter Hopps, the Corcoran director, sent me there to oversee progress on the models and drawings for the exhibition. My next contact with Soleri was in 1970 when he was installing the work in the Corcoran galleries. At one point we disagreed on how the scroll drawings should be displayed. I had remembered watching him work at Cosanti on these beautiful drawings, some sixty feet long. The disagreement became more than quite heated. Hopps told me he had no choice but to terminate me as curator, two weeks before the opening.

**SH: The book is a reflection of the period—the late 1960s and early 1970s. Typographically, it combined a curious midcentury modern aesthetic (Helvetica and Bodoni type and high-contrast imagery) with a post-Dada/futurist and "underground" press anarchy. Was this on your mind when you began to design?**

DW: Insofar as anarchy is concerned, the book was intended to be a response to the era in which it was being designed . . . the Vietnam War, the assassination of Martin Luther King Jr., the nationwide riots . . . the real-time video clips of the war. . . . I would look out my office window and see Washington burning, the sky aglow in red . . . the army bivouacked outside the architecture school. I *lived* those days of social turmoil. The art world was also in upheaval. There was a lot of anti-traditionalism happening in those days. While the New Modernism in graphic design was coming out of Boston, blueprints of Archigram's projects were being circulated via underground networks throughout schools of architecture, including illustrations of Walking City with text "walking" around the images. I listened to the Beatles' *Revolution 9* over and over. Their introduction of multi-sourced "sound montage" into music, free of lyrics, suggested the same could be done in the book but with "type montage" continuing page after page, free of narrative. With all that happening around me, I couldn't do a traditional book. I had to find a way to transfer the ferment of the day into designing *Visionary Cities*. The epoch, to me, was a time in America having an unconcluded future, marked by an uncontrollable present, with uncertainty everywhere in evidence. It galvanized me to attempt to do likewise: to create a book having an unconcluded future, possessing a seemingly uncontrollable present, with uncertainty everywhere in evidence.

As to why the use of Bodoni and Helvetica, I thought that Bodoni was visually lyrical because of the serif mode, and for this reason seemed appropriate for commentary text from a critic. Helvetica, by contrast, being without serif, I regarded as nonpersonal, lacking inflection, appropriate for fact-based biographical data. The Bodoni and the Helvetica were conceived as two "voices" engaged in discourse. The use of high-contrast photography was totally accidental. Since the Arcology models were all made of plastic, they were photographed in a dark room with a light source to illuminate the plastic, resulting in high-contrast images. This became the impetus for creating a book that was basically black. Without the photographs provided by the apprentices there would be no *Visionary Cities*.

**SH: The smashing together of type was an outcome of phototypesetting and a breaking of the classical traditions. How did you accomplish this look? Press type? Typositor?**

**DW:** Hundreds of sheets of press-type of black and white lettering were used, ranging from 6pt to 144pt. The routine was simple. For instance, pin down a photo of an Arcology, overlay it with a rigid plastic sheet, then start applying press-type, letter by letter as words, phrases, positioning them horizontally, vertically, diagonally, or any which way, all done by hand with a burnisher. Adding more text, or changing from white to black press-type, required another plastic sheet to be overlaid, and another if necessary, sometimes reaching five levels deep. Obviously text that was commercially typeset was excluded from this process, except for a few instances. The layering of text took place generally without any preplanning. Just start on one page, then see where it goes. Process was product. Must have spent hundreds of hours applying the letters with the utmost of exactitude. Kind of insane to do a book this way. As much as I've always admired Dada and Futurist typography, the immediate source of superimpositioning was Rauschenberg's 1964 sculpture *Shades*, which was made of interchangeable Plexiglas panels with lithographed images from newspapers and magazines.

**SH: How would you say that the book design represents both Soleri's work and the aesthetics and politics of the period?**

**DW:** The book contains illustrations of each period of his work, his writings, augmented by a critical essay on the Arcology thesis. Since the writings elaborate in some detail his castigating views concerning the ecological and social blight being incurred by an architecture of urban sprawl, that would have been sufficient. Instead the book's main interest lay in exploring the relationship of *wordtypographia* and the genesis thesis underpinning Soleri's Arcology.

**SH: Did you have any pushback on the design direction from the publisher?**

**DW:** The contract I signed with Praeger gave me total control over all text, imagery, layout and design of the book which, according to my editor Brenda Gilchrist, they'd never done before. When I brought the dummy sheets to New York for review with Brenda and the publisher, I did get resistance from some of the staff. The salespeople said the book was not sellable because nobody's going to take a book with an eight-page foldout and read it on the subway. The technical staff said you can't do all those foldouts like that. I said, Why not? You take the signatures. You glue one foldout to one signature and another foldout to the adjacent signature. The publisher turned to them and asked if it was possible. They said, "Yes . . . we suppose so. But we've never done that before." The publisher said, "Do it. I want this one for the Frankfurt Book Fair."

**SH: Did you design any books subsequent to this one?**

**DW:** I haven't designed any other books since *Visionary Cities*. I edited a book on the painter Gene Davis in 1975. I'm working on two books now, *Revisiting Dennis Oppenheim* and *The Backstory to the Making of* Visionary Cities.

I would like to mention that certain aspects of *Visionary Cities* appeared earlier in the boxed catalog Documenta that the Corcoran published for the Soleri Retrospective. This was a 10" × 10" × 11" cardboard box that contained sixteen scroll drawings stacked in an egg crate, on top of which sat an eighty-four-page booklet. Also in 1970 Praeger published an interim softcover version of *Visionary Cities*.

**SH: Other than its status in design history as representing expressionistic book typography, what do you think is the most important (or innovative) aspect of the book?**

**DW:** When I wrote *Visionary Cities*, books on architecture were mainly a compilation of photographs of buildings, elevations, floor plans, perhaps accompanied by a critical essay. The format was traditional and standard: text, illustrations with captions underneath. *Visionary Cities* threw all that out. At first reading, the book seems rife with arbitrarily placed lettering. Fragments of words, snippets of commentary appearing everywhere resulted in visual litter. Some photographs may not have been captioned, or the captions often were shoved into a corner of a page in a font so small it verged on the insignificant. Often illustrations were accompanied by superimposed text that obliterated, seemingly without cause.

To understand why all this is happening, it is critical that a reader must understand, even at a cursory level, the role of the invented *genesis* thesis extracted from Soleri's writings, one that postulates the evolution of mankind's consciousness, stage by stage, and how his architecture exemplifies each stage of evolution. In terms of design, the genesis thesis organizes the entire book from layout strategy, to editing and sequence of content, the visual and conceptual composition of each page, to exploring subject matter as wordtypographia. I transposed the thesis graphically into a half-page format. It begins with the word "premise" and outlines the evolutionary stages of mankind's consciousness. Each stage describes an architecture that correlates factually and philosophically with the genesis thesis. The first stage is the gaseous Undimensional, followed by the 1 Dimensional Extended expressed in his bridges, which in terms of book design allowed "extension" to be manifested by a foldout thirty inches in length. The 2 Dimensional involves the "Cosmic Potentials" that harness alternative energy produced by the sun and wind. Mesa City, being a transition from the 2D to the 3D, is simulated by a foldout eighty inches in length, reinforcing the 1 Dimensional Extended. This substantiates further the book's identity as an object in real time and space. The genesis graphic occurs some seventeen times over the run of the book. Each time new information is either added or deleted or undergoes emphasis. Understanding the genesis thesis is cumulative. It reaches a graphic complexity in the 3 Dimensional Arcology.

However, to validate the genesis thesis, the book had to include what was happening in the Undimensional. But Soleri didn't do an architecture that correlates to the chaotic Undimensional. The problem was solved by taking photographs of his Solimene Ceramica Factory in Vietri sul Mare, Italy, on top of which was superimposed type of all sizes, fonts, densities, positions, legibility, and fragmentation, to induce a visual sense of chaos. Also a seemingly irrational intrusion occurs by the numeral 1 repeated twenty-two times at an angle, charging across from one edge of the page to the other, further adding to the sense of the chaotic. Since 1 reappears throughout the book, it raises the question: "Why does an attribute of one of the stages appear in another stage?"

The answer, according to the genesis thesis, is: *Every stage in the evolutionary process contains within itself the preceding stage.* And so . . . visual chaos came into existence, like sin, destined to be present at every stage of evolution, including the Arcological. This dictum of absorption of each stage into the next culminates by the end of the book in a frenzied montage of disputing commentary.

# HOW TO DRAW
# WHAT TO DRAW

--- --- --- --- --- --- --- --- --- ---

## INTERVIEW WITH
## PETER BLEGVAD

--- --- --- --- --- --- --- --- --- --- ---

**A**pproximately forty-give-or-take-a-year-or-two years ago, I met Peter Blegvad at 7:00 a.m., my usual portfolio review time, in my *New York Times* office. Although we were both bleary eyed, I was as impressed with his range of work—comic strips (he created the strip *Leviathan*), illustration, music—then as I am today. Born in the United States, he's lived in England for most of his life, so I was taken with the hybrid American timbre mixed with London intonation. He assumed the role of a philosopher-artist for whom traditional pen-and-ink illustration was a means to an end. However, I'm not exactly certain whether he knew or found that end then or now. I'm always getting copies of his recent endgames in the mail. Three years ago it was *Gonwards*, a boxed set of CDs and DVDs, last year it was two books in one, *Milano Eagles & The Marvelous Moo*, which took forty years to make and its byline reads Björn d'Algevey, an exquisite corpse of Blegvad and the late Pushpin Studios illustrator-storyteller Jerry Joyner.

This year Blegvad sent me another type of surprise altogether that is a small part art book, an even smaller part memoir, and mostly a treatise (more like a treat) that serves as therapy for him and mind expansion for readers. The poetically enigmatic title says it all: *Imagine, Observe, Remember*; it is a book about process, memory, remembrance, and interpretation. "When I began doing comparative drawings of things imagined, observed and remembered, I was an illustrator looking for a story to illustrate. Something with a beginning, middle and end," Blegvad writes in his foreword or "Disjecta Membra" (scattered fragments) of *Imagine, Observe, Remember* . . . "It began as a way to think about illustration. It became a way of using illustration to think about imagining, observing and remembering. It's a kind of phenomenology project, a way to look at different ways of looking and seeing, using the means at my disposal, using myself as subject." After reading it twice, I thought it would be nice if Blegvad provided insight into this practical theoretical philosophical wonderment.

**Steven Heller: You write that the book "became a way of using a kind of phenomenology project, a way to look at different ways of looking and seeing using the means at my disposal, using myself as subject." Does this mean that it is a memoir or something other?**

**Peter Blegvad:** There are bits of memoir interspersed throughout, but the book is something very "other." The writer Sally O'Reilly says it's "like theory fiction crossed with a graphic novel; and other than Paul Klee's notebooks, I can't think of anything else quite like it." It starts like a memoir, looking back to when I began the project, forty-five years ago. But as memoir it's unreliable, as memory is. The story I tell about how and why I began drawing things X 3 could be told differently, like this for instance:

*Someone once dared to ask "What's the point? Why bother to make comparative drawings of things depicted thrice?" One answer is that I was curious to see which of the three faculties—Imagination, Observation, or Memory—inspired the better drawing. (And, because I doubted my ability to draw well, I adopted a pseudoscientific approach in order that my work might transcend critical evaluation on purely aesthetic grounds. I wanted to escape the tyranny of criticism, including self-criticism.)*

In the book I describe how the basic idea of drawing things X 3—imagined, observed, remembered—was inspired by my struggle to develop a style as an illustrator. I liked accurate mimetic drawings, based on observation, but I also liked distortion, abstraction, and stylization, based more on imagination and memory. So I was experimenting with these different approaches, drawing things as I pictured them mentally and then drawing them again from life, in order to help me decide which approach to follow. As I grew more adept at drawing my mental images of things, I began to find them as interesting, in their flawed imperfect way, as the things they were images of. So gradually my focus shifted from thinking about illustration to using illustration to think about how we imagine, observe, and remember.

There's also a memoir-like section about my parents—Erik and Lenore Blegvad—who were both artists and who were my primary influences.

The sections devoted to my own experiments aren't exactly memoirs, but as records of past activity there's an aspect of that to them.

But other sections of the book are based on workshops I taught over the years and are concerned with visualization exercises for writers and illustrators, with hypnagogic vision, with the poetics of failure, with encyclopaedias, with ancient Greek mnemonic techniques, with the history of cognitive science and eccentric figures like Sir Francis Galton, the Victorian polymath who's probably mainly infamous now as the founder of eugenics, but who was also a pioneer psychonaut who performed strange experiments on himself in order to catch a glimpse of his own mental processes at work. I like the problems that arise when the mind tries to observe itself. It's a conundrum, like trying to taste your own tongue. It might be impossible, but one can proceed *as if* it wasn't.

So, I'd say the book is less a memoir than an extended Surrealist experiment designed to encourage the idea of using oneself as a laboratory.

**SH: There is a large amount of philosophical discourse with yourself. What are the main questions you want to answer? And what have you succeeded or failed in answering?**

**PB:** Questions: What is real? What isn't? Where does the life live? Is it necessary to forget in order to imagine? What is the nature of the phenomena one "sees" with the mind's eye? What is the nature of this "seeing"? How might such phenomena be translated into visible images? What is lost, what is gained in the process? How do we know—or think we know—what we think? Do we discover or create— observe or imagine—mental images? What moral obligation—if any—does imagination have to truth?

To me, these aren't just questions; they're mysteries. Where does the life live? One answer might be: mystery is where the life lives. The mind—consciousness—is a mystery, maybe the deepest. Nabokov said, consciousness "is the only real thing in the world and the greatest mystery of all." A question I ask more than once: What's the point? Instead of an answer I quote Jenny Diski: "Perhaps the point of asking questions is not to receive an answer but to reiterate and refine the question itself. I'm inclined to think that there is, essentially, only one question. It is 'What is the point?' and in some form or another it is asked over and over again by those of us who have failed to mature enough to stop asking it."

**SH: I've not read a book that dives as deep into the weeds as this, what triggered you to delve so deeply?**

**PB:** Curiosity, perversity, excitement at the discoveries I was making. Over forty-five years one thing led to another. I began very much with the sense of it being a lifelong labor. I needed some monumental encyclopaedic mission to distract and protect me from the void—my "self"—and maybe to precipitate a "second birth," because the first hadn't quite done the trick. It worked, more or less . . .

**SH: You write: "Although much of my work has been in black and white, color will be examined in different lights." What as an artist is first and foremost important about color?**

**PB:** That bit now reads: "Color will be examined in different lights, especially the indeterminate colour of dreams and mental images." Color is another mystery, like music. When I use color in an illustration it's often merely pragmatic, a way to direct the viewer's eye. And, if I'm lucky, to create mood, atmosphere. I'm married to a brilliant colorist, the painter Chloë Fremantle. Most of the little I know about color I've absorbed from her. I guess what's important might be to do with the energies colors generate in us. A good colorist knows how one color affects another, and how they affect us psychologically and emotionally by their harmony or dissonance. Looking at Hilma af Klint's large abstractions, for instance, is like taking a bath in color, it's exhilarating, energizing, purifying somehow.

**SH: How does _Everyman's Encyclopedia_ operate in the way you think and make?**

**PB:** Part of the appeal this project has for me is its encyclopaedic scope. As kids, many of us experienced a "nostalgia for the infinite." I never grew out of it. But I relate to the "perverse post-Enlightenment desire . . . to attempt the encyclopaedic and at the same time run it aground" identified by Swiss artist duo Fischli and Weiss (in an article by Randy Kennedy in the *New York Times*, February 2, 2016, "Fischli and Weiss: Anarchy at the Guggenheim").

In 1985 I used an old copy of *Everyman's Encyclopaedia* (the 1932 edition) as the source for a series of drawings of things beginning with 'L' imagined, observed, remembered. Laburnum, Liszt, Loch Lomond, Lion . . . These are all reproduced in the book. Why "L"? No particular reason. For the L of it. But I liked the air of obsolescence the images in the encyclopaedia had. I tried to imbue my drawings with some of their penumbral mystique.

**SH: Is it possible to see things that are not there? Other than hallucination, that is?**

**PB:** I think most of us do it all the time without being aware, and the ability—the awareness—can be "educated" (trained). Eva Brann said, "our mental life is almost continuously filled with images, noticed or unnoticed (where unnoticed does not necessarily mean unconscious, but merely unattended to)," in *The World of the Imagination: Sum and Substance*. In my experience, noticing and attending to these things can be rewarding in unpredictable ways. Because they're mysterious, and, as said, mystery is where the life lives.

Robert Irwin said, "Once you let them in, you've already done the first and most critical thing, you've honored that information by including it. And by doing that you've actually changed the world. It's nothing mystical, but you've redefined the world for yourself."

As I say in the book, you may not be able to converse with the ghost of a flea while sketching its portrait like William Blake did, but your capacity for seeing things that aren't there can be demonstrated by visualising a capital letter N and rotating it ninety degrees clockwise. What letter is it now?

**SH: What is what you call "a memory ghost"? Do we all have them or just a lucky few?**

**PB:** They're most commonly people from one's past, but one can be haunted by sensations, by sounds, by language, or by objects too—a remembered room or house, for instance, or the car you rode in as a child. Some people are haunted by old phone numbers or mathematical equations. There can't be many people—except maybe the very young—who aren't haunted by something or someone from time to time.

# I LOVE TYPOGRAPHY, THE STORE

## INTERVIEW WITH NADINE CHAHINE

**"I** Love Typography," an influential voice in the world of type, letters, and typography, just launched an innovative web shop "dedicated to font discovery and licensing." It promises to be a fair and equitable, accessible and spirited means for an ever-increasing number of typeface designers (and graphic designers who design typefaces) and foundries to distribute their wares. To help celebrate the launch, some of the world's most respected type designers are releasing new faces and launching new foundries that will be represented on the site. ILT is christening 16 fresh typefaces, and they have 40 foundries on board for almost 7,000 fonts total. The plan is to grow "very quickly."

The three founders of this long-in-the-making venture include CCO John Boardley, a type historian, critic, and blogger who has amassed almost half a million Twitter followers. Meanwhile, CRO Julia Hiles brings more than 20 years' sales leadership experience in both the finance and creative industries. Hiles will center this creative ecosystem around sustainable business models that benefit both foundries and brands: "In a corporate world where everyone starts to look the same, brand owners can turn to us to discover the right brand expression, confident in the knowledge that they are licensing high-quality typefaces that are fit for purpose," she says.

ILT's CEO is veteran typologist Dr. Nadine Chahine; she combines expertise in type design, legibility, and international relations to steer ILT in its new expansion. Named one of *Fast Company*'s "100 Most Creative People in Business" in 2012 and *Creative Reviews*' "Creative Leaders 50" in 2016, Chahine is focused on empowering independent foundries and creating a customer experience that is rooted in the joy of discovering and licensing new fonts. "Finding the right typeface for your project should not be a chore," she says. "There is such a storm of expressions in type design and we want to bring that diversity and power into the hands of designers. We also want to create a platform where independent foundries can thrive and maintain control of their business models. We believe that such a twin-speared approach can help foster a creative ecosystem that celebrates the beauty of the written word."

I asked Chahine to explain at greater length just why ILT will be beneficial for type makers, type users, and type audiences.

**SH: A year ago the website and blog *I Love Typography* launched a unique web shop platform dedicated to "font discovery" and licensing. What are its unique features and services?**

NC: A unique feature that we have is our system of type descriptors, CEDARS+, which helps transform font discovery from endless scrolling into an enjoyable experience. The name is an acronym for contrast, energy level, details, rhythm, axis, and structure. The plus is for script specific features. This system allows us to describe a typeface based on its formal characteristics and to use these as powerful filters. So for example, if you are working on branding for racing bikes, you could go onto CEDARS+ and select high energy and low contrast. You could do that search for Latin typefaces or for any of the other scripts we support. CEDARS+ also allows for the type of granular search such as when you are looking for a specific serif that you have in mind for a book title. Or you are looking for an M for a logo where that midpoint is floating rather than on the baseline.

Another unique aspect is the set of social features that we allow on the site. A user can follow foundries for their updates. They can favorite fonts so as to come back to them later. You know, this is not rocket science. These are social features that one can easily expect based on how we live our online lives today. It's just that the major font distributors have not really looked to the outside world in quite a long time.

**SH: You are all veterans in the realm of type design, font marketing, and type design advocacy; there must have been tipping points that pushed your venture. What are you hoping and planning to improve in the font universe?**

NC: It all came together last autumn when I was preparing to launch my first foundry collection and there was no font distributor that I felt comfortable with. I could not trust my fonts with my previous employers for all the reasons that made me leave that employment and the others on the market did not appear to have shaken the monopoly that currently chokes our industry. If anything, that is our biggest driver. To offer a breathing space for foundries to exist and flourish, a space that is driven by the wish to sustain our industry and to ensure its continuity. For designers and foundries and the creative spirit that binds us.

**SH: What do you feel have been the flaws and faults in the font distribution and marketing system for both creators and users?**

NC: For many years now the same phenomenon repeats itself: you release a typeface after a lot of hard work, it gets its moment in the sun, and then it disappears. It's extremely difficult for a foundry to promote a new typeface. For the users of type, there are so many typefaces out there, it is really difficult to navigate that space. Imagine all the typefaces in existence today; they are all floating in a very deep well, and only the ones at the surface get to see the light. Everything else sinks to the bottom. Our aim is to transform that well into a clear and shallow lake where the light of the sun shines all the way through. In that transformation we find that typographic choice goes beyond the typographic styles that get used all the time, that there is such a joy in exploring those blue waters.

**SH: How is the new font platform different from others? I presume you'd call them, and notably, Fonts in Use, the competition?**

**NC:** We are the only ones who started off with great content that celebrates the beauty of type, and then decided to make that type directly accessible to everyone! ILT was never meant to be a business venture, but a place for John to speak about the topic he is so passionate about. I certainly never thought I would be getting into distribution either. Our motivation is coming from our positions within our community, the responsibility that brings, and a sense of common purpose. Furthermore, our competitors are font distributors. What we are building is a creative ecosystem that includes font distribution as well as great content, social features, and a host of other capabilities that we are still building. There is so much more to do still!

**SH: You have said that "some of the world's best type designers are releasing new typefaces, and launching new foundries, in celebration" of your launch, translating into sixteen new typefaces, and have forty foundries on board with almost seven thousand fonts. There has obviously been a lot of prep work. How long has this first stage been going on? Why has it been shrouded in secrecy?**

**NC:** We started discussing this in October 2020 and got to work on it in earnest in November. We've worked with lightning speed to get to launch less than nine months later. Given how the font business has been evolving in the past couple of years, and that we were all unhappy with that trend, we felt a sense of urgency that this project needs to come to fruition sooner rather than later. When we spoke to foundries, we saw the same thoughts and feelings echoed by so many, which is why we have had this wave of unprecedented support to our cause. The foundries have been magnificent! That we are now able to celebrate the launch together is in many ways testament to their willingness to jump into the trenches with us and to stand with us shoulder to shoulder as we build this site for all of us.

**SH: What is the incentive for designers and foundries to collaborate with you at this point in time?**

**NC:** What I heard in every call I made was a deep sense of unhappiness and frustration with the status quo. Couple that with all the ideas we have on how to change things and the result is not surprising. We bring an innovative approach to the way of distributing fonts that has not changed in fifteen years and I hope that once they look at the site, even when it is taking its baby steps, they will see how far we plan to go.

**SH: Indeed, what will established and startup foundries gain?**

**NC:** Trust, openness, and transparency.

**SH: How will you "curate" or decide who to represent? And will this be an exclusive relationship with each supporting "member"?**

**NC:** Good design done by good people! However, in this first round we do not have a wide enough reach whether in geographic representation, the number of scripts we offer, or the background of designers we feature. So these are our next areas of expansion and they will affect the choices of who to invite next.

**SH: What have you learned from your long stint as an expert at Monotype that underpins your innovations?**

**NC:** I learned that middle managers kill speed and efficiency and that it is essential that the leadership understands type in order to serve that industry well.

**SH: When the Mac was introduced in 1984 I called it a digital type revolution in the making. I've watched how different font companies and type foundries have come and gone as that revolution picked up steam. Are you signaling another unprecedented shift or are you more modestly improving on what exists?**

**NC:** It is such a compliment to be seen in such light, thank you! I don't know, to be honest. It's certainly a revolution in its spirit, and I want to leapfrog us into the future. When I read what John writes, and hear Julia's advice on font business, it feels like there is nothing we cannot do. But this is what is in our hearts. What we need to do is the hard work of proving that we are up for the task, and that the ideas we bring forth are salient. I don't know how that will turn out but we certainly intend to work really hard to push for the type of change we want to see happen.

**SH: What does the future have in store for the type world?**

**NC:** The worst-case scenario: a couple of acquisitions that could drive small independent foundries out of business and turn the font industry into a subscription/ free service where a few are able to flourish, and the rest are decimated. Where no newcomers will ever be able to sustain a career as a type designer. The horrific crashing of the type design ecosystem.

The sunnier scenario: We have a thriving ecosystem filled with the celebration of the beauty of type and the joy of font exploration, powered by the speed of innovation, and creating a cycle of growth that sustains our creative industry.

We will do everything we can to push for the better scenario. The foundries have shown that they will too.

# PART 6:
# TYPE LOVE

# THE TYPEFACE THAT WAS ONCE THE FUTURE

- - - - - - - - - - - - - - - - -

"The Type of Today and Tomorrow" is the catchy slogan the Bauer Type Foundry office in New York coined to announce the release of Futura, Paul Renner's 1927 geometric sans serif, in the United States. There were other popular homegrown and imported sans serifs available in the United States, including Jakob Erbar's Erbar (1922), Rudolf Koch's Kabel (1927), W. A. Dwiggins's Metro (1927), Lucian Bernhard's Bernhard Gothic (1929) and others, but neither these nor other typefaces at the time were as comparably geometric as was Futura.

Introduced in the United States in 1928 only a couple of years before the onset of the Great Depression, as a metal font type family of various size and weight variations its release was promoted with the fanfare of specimen sheets showing the type in use—a very common marketing practice during that period. These specimens emphasized Futura's starched, modern look and how well it functioned in large and small sizes in many contexts. It had incredible appeal, in large part because Futura did not revive an existing typeface yet it was not so radically loud as to overpower a message.

Most American advertisements used sans serif typefaces that were either bold condensed or bold expanded. With Futura, ad typography was effectively altered from conventional to novel. Even the name "Futura" had such allure that it quickly became one the most popular typefaces for years until Helvetica was created.

There was no more influential advocate for Futura in the United States than *Vanity Fair* magazine, Condé Nast's cosmopolitan culture, art, and literary monthly. In 1929 its venturesome art director, Ukraine-born Dr. Mehemed Fehmy Agha, not only introduced Futura as the only display face in the magazine, he also removed all capital letters in *Vanity Fair*'s headlines. The result was at once jarring yet elegantly modern.

The lowercase "experiment," which lasted only five issues, helped define *Vanity Fair*'s progressive design. However, while suddenly the capitals disappeared, suddenly they reappeared in the March 1930 issue in which the editors published an editorial titled, "A Note on Typography." Although the case was more important than the face in this context, the editors implied that this trial was best done with a face representing the New Typography of the European avant-garde.

"Typography without capital letters was introduced in Europe soon after the Great War and has been working westward ever since," the editors wrote.

FOR THE LOVE OF DESIGN

"It has not been used so much in text, but in all situations where the value of display is paramount it has been extremely popular. Thus, the intense competition of advertising, where the least optical advantage makes itself felt at once, has already made some modern typography familiar to Americans."

This passage was followed by particularly astute raison d'etre for Futura to have been designed in the first place: "Any art, particularly any art with a function as utilitarian as that of typography, consciously or unconsciously conforms itself in the peculiar temper of the living and contemporary civilization."

In an explanation of how experimental typography is an adaptive force, the editors wrote: "An innovation stands out at first like a sore thumb but before it has passed its infancy it has become invisible to the conscious eye. . . . In using, and continuing to use, the new typography, *Vanity Fair* believes that it knows very well what it is doing. In modifying one of the conventions of the new typography by returning to the use of capital letters in titles, it is obeying considerations that outlast any mere 'revolution in style.' The issue is thus one between attractiveness and legibility, or between form and content, and *Vanity Fair*, not wishing to undertake a campaign of education, casts its vote by returning to the use of capital letters in titles, to legibility, and to the cause of content above form."

The general readership to who this statement was aimed did not buy typefaces but they were made aware of it and gleaned a bit of typographic literacy. For the designers and production managers who did buy and use type, Futura was promoted in the United States by articles and examples in *PM/AD*, *American Printer*, and *PRINT* magazines, but almost nothing was more impressive than seeing it in *Vanity Fair*.

Paul Rand's typeface preferences included various modern san serifs, from Trade Gothic to Helvetica—and even A. M. Cassandre's Peignot just once, the first time it appeared in the United States—and Futura Bold was frequently used in advertisements and books designed during the 1940s. Among these, Rand's typographical ad for Benzedrine featured a Futura Bold lowercase b enlarged to fill the page. Thanks to its near perfect geometry, this Futura letterform was very startling when scaled-up to such huge proportions.

For a series of Stafford Fabrics ads, Rand spaced out lowercase Futura Bold letters in the company's name, and used the same type in smaller sizes for both headline and text on all the company's advertisements. The Futura Bold letters were printed in alternating colors, paired with abstract photo illustrations, and projected an air of modernity. Similarly, the Futura Bold lowercase title jazzways, the nameplate for a hybrid book-magazine, perfectly complemented Rand's Paul Klee–inspired symbolic cover illustration of four abstracted musical instruments that suggested modern jazz. Rand also widely spaced out Futura Bold on the title page for a book of Hans Arp's poems and essays. The letters a-r-p virtually dance on the page.

Despite the frequency with which Futura was used, it was not Rand's favorite typeface, and he grew tired of it by the mid-1950s. He much preferred the classic Bodoni instead.

Futura was introduced in the United States prior to the Czech designer Ladislav Sutnar's 1939 arrival in New York City. Yet its status increased more after Sutnar established it as one of the most emblematic typefaces for industrial and trade catalogs, which he designed from 1941 to 1960, produced by the Sweet's Catalog Service.

Sutnar preferred lowercase Futura Bold and Medium, owing to functionality, legibility, and personality. In his opus *Catalog Design Progress* Futura is the typographic complement to his obsessive application of geometric icons as chapter markers and subject tabs. The typeface was part of an equation that also included shape, color, and line that equaled what Sutnar called "'traffic signs that quickly transmit the identifying information" to the users of Sweet's respective catalogs.

Sutnar was not a late adopter, but rather a Futura devotee while still working in Czechoslovakia, designing book and magazine covers starting in 1929 for Drustevní Prace, Prague's largest publishing house. Although Sutnar was a prolific writer on design process, he never wrote explicitly on the virtues of Futura, but the face conformed to his basic credo of what he referred to as good visual design: "Its aim is not to attain popular success by going back to the nostalgia of the past, or by sinking to the infantile level of a mythical public taste," he wrote. And Futura was a typeface that never was passé.

# A TYPE CATALOG LEGACY

-- -- -- -- -- -- -- -- -- -- -- -- -- -- -- -- --

**T**he end of mass-market commercial letterpress printing in the second half of the twentieth century was also the death knell of metal and wood type founding as a flourishing industry. After five hundred years, the movable type revolution gave way to photocomposition and then (if you don't count press-type) to digital typefaces in various programmatic incarnations, which reduced the need for factory-foundries to computer screens. "Physically, the only remaining vestige of an American foundry," wrote Maurice Annenberg in *Type Foundries of America and Their Catalogs* (originally published in 1975 in an edition of five hundred and reprinted in 1994 by Oak Knoll Press), "could be an old warn type catalog."

A commercial printer who had an early interest in studying and chronicling the history of his profession, Annenberg (1907–1979) collected a substantial library of rare printing manuals, journals, and type specimen books that serve among the raw materials of design history—and are today both treasured and fetishized. "The artists and designers of the present century," Annenberg wrote over forty years ago, "now find these catalogs extremely valuable in tracing old alphabets to be used as a pattern in creating 'new' typefaces using the photo distortion camera."

When his extensive research into America's foundries and their catalogs was first published, Annenberg noted that printing arts librarians reported that the pilfering of vintage catalogs had increased tenfold during the 1970s over previous decades. Type and graphic designers realized their value as an original resource for exotic and eccentric fonts was garnering new appreciation, resulting in the emergence of classical revivals and contemporary retro graphics. Type vendors like Morgan Press and Tri-Arts sold antique nineteenth-century wood and metal types, while Dover Publications, among others, published clip art books filled with copyright-free reproductions of pages containing full or partial alphabets and a wide range of printing ornaments taken directly from the original foundry specimens.

Decades earlier, sample books were routinely given freely to customers as part of their printing toolkits offered by foundries, which in addition to type included presses, binding and folding machines, and other hardware. These books were so heavy that sales agents often complained about having to carry so many. New ones were kept and old ones discarded since they took up so much space. Eventually, large books gave way to sheets and brochures. Few at the time could predict that the specimen books would eventually become rare, expensive artifacts. (In fact, twice during the early 1970s I was given the opportunity to sift through the stores of catalog and specimen libraries from two failed printing companies that had no further need for their respective hoards. One of them simply left the material in a flatbed truck parked for a week on a street in lower Manhattan.)

Yet not all these materials were summarily trashed. Columbia University in New York purchased the American Type Founders (ATF) library in 1941. Begun in 1908, the 1923 ATF catalog summed up the importance of their archive this way: "The collections in the library include type specimen books and broadsides from 1486 to the present time. . . . The Typographic Library and Museum assumes the duty of collecting and preserving the memorabilia of printing and printers of all nations."

Type specimen books are wellsprings of all kinds of sociohistorical (and even political) documentation. The late nineteenth century, for example, was the early era of what could be seen as "capitalist modern" printing in most industrialized nations of the world. Type foundries were integral to the publishing of information but also to selling goods and services through advertising and packaging. Type was not just a means, as it was in Gutenberg's time, for efficiently propagating religious teachings or later in making government decrees and bureaucratic declarations. Nor were books and magazines the primary customers as literacy increased. The rise of industry and spread of commerce created a need for an entire printing industry and, of course, distinctive type designs played a large role in articulating the importance of business and joys of consumption.

Type itself became a competitive business and the majority of late nineteenth- and early twentieth-century catalogs were designed to sell. Typical of the kind of sales text in specimen books is the following from an obscure New York foundry, Adorinam Chandler & Co., which Annenberg stated "is obscured in type founding history and the only tangible legacy is his type catalog," which announced in a preface that "The ornamental types exhibited in this specimen are cast in stereotypical plates, and the letter separately fixed to wooden bottoms . . . Printers are left to judge for themselves, whether it is not a saving to buy this, instead of giving forty-two cents per pound for type metal." And the following from the 1893 Boston-based Dickenson Type Foundry book announced in type that was "cast from Copper Alloy Metal," the "Lightest and most durable in the world" claimed "The arrangement and printing of these pages is the result of necessary haste, but we bespeak the leniency of their printer when considering these imperfections in connection with the large labor involved."

Catalogs made clear to customers that while their faces may not be the latest fashions, it is reliable. From the Western Type Foundry in Chicago and St. Louis in 1909 comes this: ". . . whenever you see the name WESTERN TYPE—it is as good as the type made by the foundries 20 years ago. . . . Better material was never made than that which goes into WESTERN TYPE."

The problem with publishing specimen books was keeping up with the newly designed faces. The Inland Type Foundry preface from 1906 asserted: "The printing of a specimen book requires time, and the Inland Type Foundry produces new face with such rapidity that a new edition was scarcely off the press until it was, to some extent, obsolete, as one or more faces had been produced while the book was going thru the press." It added that "The experiment was tried of issuing supplements, but this was found unsatisfactory. Often they were received by people who thought them to be ordinary circulars and threw them in the wastebasket." The answer, they realized, was a loose-leaf volume for updates—so innovative that Inland wrote: "We particularly request that you designate some person who shall receive these supplements and show who shall have positive instructions to place them in the book as soon as they come to hand. . . . [and] promptly send us the name of this person."

One specimen book generally looked a lot like another, though each handled samples differently. In *Alphabets To Order: The Literature of Nineteenth-Century Typefounders' Specimens* (2000), type historian and printer Alastair Johnston analyzes the typographic/word juxtapositions in scores of catalogs. For example, the line "HAMBURGH Beautiful Sierras" was on the same page as "ARTISTIC SELECTION / The Modern Sciences 2567." In another, Chicago's Union Type Foundry, "MONOPLE RARE / CHANCE TIDBITS / 23 MERE 62" seems like an arbitrary selection with a touch of absurdist modern poetry.

One of my favorite combinations was an 1894 ad for Inland with the headline "This Is Not Pi" set in a rash of different faces. For those who don't know the term, pi is when a case or chase is accidentally dropped and all the types are a mess of mixed-up sizes. This ad is reminiscent of the Futurist and Dada typographic mischief that began more than a decade later.

Type specimen books for some young designers are vestiges, while for others they are gems of legacy. The era of this kind of elaborate bibles of typeface design is long over as it should be; digital times require digital samples with "test-drive" capacity and other type-manipulating software (like http://metapolator.com/home/). Still some digital foundries continue to produce paper specimen sheets and posters, if only to pay homage to the past, and to leave an analog collectible behind. Still, like the bibles they were, paging through a vintage type book is a mix of religious and ecstatic experience.

# TYPEFACES IN REVIEW

------

### Erotique – Zetafonts.com

The word *erotic* derives from the Greek erōs, which springs from mythic god Eros, the mischievous representation of carnal love. The word erotique is French. Must I say more? Oui ou non?

Erotic implies arousal of senses; a certain furtive pleasure. Yet I make no secret of getting pleasure from Erotique, Zetafonts.com's new—*trés chic*—type family.

Zetafonts claims the following: "Typography has never been sexier." Maybe! Maybe not? I am attracted by the alluring sensuality of typeface's evocative serifs and the assemblage of sinuous heavy and light strokes in various of its upper- and lowercase letters that suggests the coupling of both calligraphic and cursive characteristics. Far and above, for me, the most stimulating aspects of Erotique are the exotique ribbon-like tail of the Q and the exquisite swirl of the lowercase ligatures. The caps are similar to and yet do not mimic Bodoni. I am inspired by the particularly nuanced serifs of the "C" and "W" and the curlicues of the ethereal alternative "A," "E," and "X." To my eye the lowercase Erotique Monoline, Regular, Medium and Bold, notably have the most personality as a combo roman and script. I particularly appreciate the curved bowl of the "t."

As promiscuous as Erotique appears, its decided complexity, which is so transfixing, also has limitations. You might say Erotique is a stylish dress suit, not a practical sports coat that can be worn only at classy occasions.

It will be difficult to pair Erotique with most other faces. This is why it is best used as a headline, masthead or logo—something that basks in the spotlight. As a text face, it impresses a unique texture on a block of text; however, it is difficult not to be distracted by its whimsical unconventionality.

Nonetheless this family does live up to its quixotic name—it is romantic and fanciful with a soupçon of dreamy irregularity.

### Oposta – DSType

I found myself hypnotically charmed by Oposta for various logical and visceral reasons, much in the same way I am attracted by the sensual streamline of a 2022 BMW 8 series convertible. Obviously, there is no commonsensical link between this extremely expanded slab serif typeface and the bullet-nosed high-performance Bavarian Motors automobile, but there is a common sensation. I admit to having BMWs on the brain these days, and Oposta conjures up the sleek perfection of a smartly proportioned (and exquisitely photographed) one. I'd like to test-drive both.

The allure comes from the fact that every top and bottom slab is precisely in sync with the letter adjacent to it. Picture the word JULY, for instance, the upper slabs fit together geometrically as one. The lower bowls of the J, U, Y have sensual balance. As complex as the letterforms are, simplicity nonetheless reigns.

The thin lines on the lower a, e, p, y are delicate to the extreme. Magically, the upper and lower cases flawlessly combine to form distinct units. Then there is the most ingeniously designed characteristic of all: When composed as words in sentences, the midpoint of each letter aligns to suggest a straight line that is slashed through the center of each setting. This is arguably one of the most dynamic conceits I've ever seen—and no small design feat either.

Exaggerated heavy Italianate nineteenth-century slab serifs were revived during the 1960s psychedelic era; they were designed to ebb and flow, and their shifting contours achieved dreamlike effects. Oposta is the opposite of that. It is meant to be set in continuous blocks, in solid darks and lights, and as if compressed into an inflexible mass of words.

The wonderful part is that it reads perfectly well. Each letter and therefore every word is entirely legible. There are no encumbrances to thwart meaning or understanding. That is, if you don't veer away and fixate on how beautiful the Oposta O is. The horizontal inner oval is so gorgeous, like a squinting eye in every word in which it appears. The O is my favorite letter, that is if you don't count the lowercase r; it is the joining of square, rectangle, line, and half circle that always triggers a smile.

//////

### Valvolina – Device Fonts

I am somewhat perplexed why designers like myself are seduced by the streamlined styles of Italian Futurist-era type and typography? Are revivals like this month's selection, Valvolina (Device Fonts), appealing as radically aesthetic alternatives to classical Italian letters? Does Valvolina's thrusting, geometric angularity evoke a radical ethos of motion and energy? Does it suggest today or yesterday?

Perhaps I am reading too much into it. Valvolina (which borrows the name from a motor oil) is not symbolic at all but rather has startling resonance on a page or screen. Or as Sigmund Freud might have said, "often a typeface is just a typeface." This sharp-edge-abstract sans serif has sparked other appropriations, notably Milton Glaser's 1968 Baby Teeth (the only type used on his famous "Dylan" poster), which he had originally found on a sign in Mexico and was a popular display face there. During the 1920s and 1930s, Italian foundries released similar hand-drawn wood and metal iterations.

So, unless my eyes and memory deceive me, it seems that the Valvolina style may be on the verge of a new popularity inspired by its bizarre yet engaging assemblage of contrapuntal shapes; when used for display in large and small sizes it exudes a sense of modernist hieroglyphics. It also comes in an outline as well, which allows for much flexibility.

///////

**Show Family – Huy! Fonts**

"God is in the details" pronounced Ludwig Mies van der Rohe, referring to his architectural practice. The statement was ultimately adopted as twentieth-century Modernist commandment. Mies is also credited with the dictum "less is more" and from his epoch's reductive formal perspective he was correct on both counts. Modernism was dedicated to achieving perfection from the least possible but no less divine details. Nonetheless, arguably the same spirit can also be found in complex details.

This month's selection, *Show* from Huy! Fonts, is chosen precisely for its resurrected detailed complexity. For me it is infused with nostalgia for when God was represented in design by ornamentation galore. Influenced by nineteenth-century wood type, Show represents a decorative typographic style that comes from the past but is not passé. Show resembles handmade show cards and even more specifically, an elaborate sumptuous mannerism known as Fileteado, borne of an Argentine tradition of painting display letters commonly found on Buenos Aires's commercial handcarts and wagons to advertise the wares and services for sale. Filetes are painted colored linear motifs that might include floral and other natural imagery.

Although this ornamental font has limited practical applications today, don't be too quick to disregard the playful compositions built into the typeface. Huy! Fonts has made the most out of its layers of spirited details. The full assortment of component parts include Show Regular, Show Inner Shadow, Show Lines Vertical, Show Lines Diagonal, Show Stripes Up, Show Stripes Medium, Show Stripes Down, Show Half, Show Outline, Show Background, Show Shadow Two, Show Shadow, and Show Cast Shadow, which fit together resulting in various multi-chromatic, illusionary dimensional, almost infinite more-is-more possibilities.

# EPILOGUE

I love design. Not exclusively the visceral pleasure of a beautiful object or rapture for typography on superbly composed pages—although these certainly add to the joy—rather I am talking about how much design in all its forms has given me a purpose. Paul Rand famously said "design is everywhere." It is *everywhere* and everything.

It envelopes me. Everything on the desk where I am writing this epilogue is touched by the wand of the designer. The chair I sit on, the mouse I move around and the rubber pad it moves around on, all this stuff, is the result of design instinct, planning and execution. I feel it.

Design has provided me with *raisons d'etre*: Some epic, others trivial. Some began small and became big—iconic—others were intended to be monumental and never quite rose to the promise.

As for promise, when I began as a graphic designer, I don't think I had anything near promise. I did not, to my knowledge, have a vision—indeed I did not even have enough knowledge to be visionary. I recall being at sea when I was asked to design a poster. It seemed easy: select a typeface, paste (or wax) it down in such a compositionally pleasing manner that it could be understood, add color so it would stand out amidst others, and voila! After gazing proudly at my accomplishment, my blood curdled with anxiety. I realized there was more to the design than just making a "thing." Design demanded, among other attributes, notably the know-how to make great ideas into real, functional, and enviable products.

It was the awakening that although everything around me is designed, not everything is truly a design. Making something that has allure and is functional is the definition of design—note I'm not saying "good design," because what expresses these qualities should go without saying. Good design is the basis on which great design stories are written.

I've written hundreds of stories about ideas, objects, and people through the lens of design for decades. I have written about what I personally consider either to be good or meaningful. I always wonder, however, whether what I have written has done justice to both the subject and the reader. I know some of what I've done has merit, others do not. Some are critical, others are celebratory. Some are knowledgeable, others are faking it. I was recently asked by an interviewer if I had confidence in what I have to say about my subjects. At an immediate loss to respond, I said that the reason I write is to build confidence in myself, but in truth, I always ask myself a question: Is what I have to say of any value? The answer is that I don't know, but I do know this: I base what I do for the love of design. If it turns out to be useful to the reader, then it is requited love.

# ACKNOWLEDGMENTS

A mighty yell to Mets fan and woodsman Tad Crawford, publisher of Allworth Press, for his decades of support as an editor and friend. I have produced over 30 books with Tad and I'm sure not all of them have done as well as he would have liked. But he has stood with me through the highs and the lows. He has also been among the few fervent design fans and advocates in this fickle publishing industry. Thank you, Tad.

Sincere thanks to Caroline Russomanno, editor at Allworth Press, for patiently waiting for my late manuscript and shepherding it through the publishing birth canal. Much appreciated, Caroline.

I am grateful to Ezra Lee, my former student at SVA MFA Design / Designer as Entrepreneur for his beautiful cover and interior design.

Many thanks to all those who were sources for the essays and interviews herein. Without these various talents to write about there would be no book. Likewise, appreciation to the editors who worked with me on the various publications from which many of these essays were adapted: Zachary Petit at Printmag.com, Nadine Chahine at Ilovetypography.com, Betsy Vardell at DesignObserver.com, Gary Groth at Fantagraphics, Joyce Rutter Kaye at SVA, Gail Anderson at Visual Arts Press, Stephanie Plunket at the Norman Rockwell Museum, Molly Cort at RIT Press, Samira Bouabana and Angela Tillman Sperandio at Hall of Femmes, Dan Crowe at Inque, and Mara Garbuno at RM.

Sadly, I say farewell to Marshall Arisman who passed away in Spring 2022. He was a wonderful friend, great colleague, and amazing storyteller. I knew what you were saying, almost always.

Finally, thanks for the loyalty of my wonderful wife, Louise Fili, and the pride of my life, my son, Nicolas Heller (a.k.a. New York Nico). And nothing would be possible if not for SVA President David Rhodes, my patron of the applied arts.

# INDEX

## R

Rand, Paul, 85, 100, 147, 155
RCA, 85
record album cover design, 95–97
*Red Star Over Russia* (King), 129
"Rejected New Nicknames for Sean 'Puff
    Daddy' Combs" (Blitt), 54
religion, 33
Remington, R. Roger, 72–73
Renner, Paul, 146
Rhodes, David, 19, 40
Rivera, Diego, 106
robots, 116, 118–119
Russian Constructivism, 128–129

## S

San Francisco Museum of Art, 126
satire, 53–58
*SAVED: My Picture World* (Keaton), 81–82
Schoener, Allon, 125–127
School of Visual Arts (SVA), 28, 40, 57,
    61–62, 77
Scorsese, Martin, 15
self-analysis, 16–17
Shea, Ammon, 48–49
Shehab, Bahia, 120–124
Show Family, 154
Silverstein, Louis, 75
Siqueiros, David Alfaro, 106
sleep, 20–22
Snyder, Timothy, 40
social design, 117–118
Soleri, Paolo, 131–133, 135
specimen books, 150–151
speech, free, 30–31, 33–34, 36–37, 41
Standard, Paul, 111–113
Steinweiss, Alex, 95
"The Sunday Outing" (Pinkney), 89
supermarket packaging, 102–104
Sutnar, Ladislav, 72, 148
symbolism and allegory, 70

## T

Talarico, Lisa, 18
Talese, Gay, 41–42
teaching, 18–19
Thompson, Brad, 85
*Through Hell With Hiprah Hunt* (Young), 52
Tibet, 77–78

time, 9–11
Trade Gothic, 147
Trader Joe's, 102, 104
tricks, 62–63
*Trotsky: A Documentary* (King), 129
Trotsky, Leon, 130
Trump, Donald J., 36–37, 40–42, 55, 57–60,
    105
Twemlow, Alice, 19
typeface, 69, 108–113, 140–143, 146–154
    wood, 108–110
*Type Foundries of American and Their Catalogs*
    (Annenberg), 149
Typographic Library and Museum, 150
typography, 16, 146–154
tyranny, 40

## U

United States Supreme Court, 32–34

## V

Valvolina, 153–154
van der Rohe, Ludwig Mies, 154
*Vanity Fair*, 68, 106, 146
Veatch, Henry, 36
Vignelli, Massimo, 19
*Visionary Cities: the Arcology of Paolo Soleri*,
    131–135
*Visual Puns in Design: The Pun Used As a*
    *Communication Tool* (Kince), 83
Vizcom, 16

## W

Wall, Don, 131–135
war, 28–29
Wayzgoose conference, 1–9
Whole Foods, 102, 104
Wikileaks, 30
witness, expert, 32
*The World of the Imagination: Sum and Substance*
    (Brann), 139
writing, 87

## Y

Young, Art, 51–52

## Z

*Zapatistas* (Orozco), 105
Zetafonts.com, 152